THE BHAGAVAD GITA

SWAMI NIRLIPTANANDA

THE BHAGAVAD GITA

Copyright © 2008 Swami Nirliptananda

The moral right of the author has been asserted.

Apart from any fair dealing for the purposes of research or private study, or criticism or review, as permitted under the Copyright, Designs and Patents Act 1988, this publication may only be reproduced, stored or transmitted, in any form or by any means, with the prior permission in writing of the publishers, or in the case of reprographic reproduction in accordance with the terms of licences issued by the Copyright Licensing Agency. Enquiries concerning reproduction outside those terms should be sent to the publishers.

Matador
9 De Montfort Mews
Leicester LE1 7FW, UK
Tel: (+44) 116 255 9311 / 9312
Email: books@troubador.co.uk
Web: www.troubador.co.uk/matador

ISBN 978 1906510 688

A Cataloguing-in-Publication (CIP) catalogue record for this book is available from the British Library.

Front cover: Lord Krishna blowing a conch.

Mixed Sources
Product group from well-managed forests and other controlled sources
www.fsc.org Cert no. TT-COC-2082
© 1996 Forest Stewardship Council

Typeset in 12pt Bembo by Troubador Publishing Ltd, Leicester, UK
Printed in the UK by The Cromwell Press Ltd, Trowbridge, Wilts, UK

Matador is an imprint of Troubador Publishing Ltd

ACKNOWLEDGMENTS

I must express my appreciation to Swami Shiveshwarananda, Lakshmi (Rita-Maria Linnenkamp) and Clive Hambidge for proof-reading the material and Paul Lamptey for the computer layout. Without their help it would have been very difficult for me in my busy life to bring out this Bhagavad Gita – the Song of the Divine. If the message touches the heart of just one person, I will consider that as a blessing of the Lord and my Spiritual Master Acharya Pranavanandaji Maharaj whose life has been influenced by the principles of the Gita that provided the divine basis on which he established his organization to serve humanity.

CONTENTS

INTRODUCTION ix
The Religion of the Bhagavad Gita

THE BHAGAVAD GITA 1

Chapter One:	The Yoga Arjuna's Despondency	3
Chapter two:	The Yoga of Knowledge	11
Chapter Three:	The Yoga of Action	37
Chapter four:	The Yoga of Renunciation of Action in Knowledge	50
Chapter Five:	The Yoga of Renunciation	64
Chapter Six:	The Yoga of Meditation	74
Chapter Seven:	The Yoga of Knowledge and Realization	86
Chapter Eight:	The Yoga of the Imperishable Brahman	93
Chapter Nine:	The Yoga of the Highest Science and Supreme Secret	100
Chapter Ten:	The Yoga of Divine Manifestations	110
Chapter Eleven:	The Yoga of Universal Revelation	117
Chapter Twelve:	The Yoga of Devotion	127
Chapter Thirteen:	The Yoga of Discrimination between the Field and Its Knower	132

vii

Chapter Fourteen:	The Yoga of the three-fold divisions of the Gunas	141
Chapter Fifteen:	The Yoga of the Supreme Self	147
Chapter Sixteen:	The Yoga of division between the Divine and the Demonical	152
Chapter Seventeen:	The Yoga of the Threefold Shraddha	157
Chapter Eighteen:	The Yoga of Liberation by Renunciation	165

Appendix Chapter VIII 17-19   187

INTRODUCTION

THE RELIGION OF THE BHAGAVAD GITA

Man is a complex being. Unlike other creatures, there is a distinct difference in the behaviour pattern between one man and another. This makes it sometimes very difficult to understand why a person behaves as he does. The Gita attributes this to his nature. Everyone acts according to one's natural disposition. Nature sometimes forces us to do things that are contrary to our best judgement. Being conditioned by our nature we act like helpless creatures.

That being the case, the Gita first points out the reason why man finds himself in that predicament and proposes ways and means by which he can overcome this problem and be his natural self. The emphasis of the religion of the Gita is not placed totally on our dependence on God or for us to seek salvation in another world. There is a great emphasis on self-effort, on one's conduct rather than one's belief. By correct practice one achieves the right result. Basically, Gita extols the purification of one's own nature. When the nature is pure, one experiences freedom, then quite naturally there is a change in attitude because the Self is no longer conditioned by the influence of the environment.

A closer relationship between man, other creatures and God helps us to view others with a friendlier attitude. In fact the Gita mentions this experience as seeing the whole of creation in ourselves and in God. The impact of such an experience leaves no room for suspicion, distrust and hate because there will not be any discrimination between one being and another. By focussing the mind on the equality of all beings one develops friendship with all and takes delight in working for the welfare of all beings. One can not then harm another without displeasing God Who is the Friend of all.

The Gita lays more emphasis on the importance of seeing God residing in the hearts of His creation. This is regarded as real grace as it gives sanctity to the existence of all beings. As such all forms of exploitation are transgressions of the sacred Law (Dharma) which is the basis of coexistence and by which everyone is protected.

Removal of suffering is one of the basic reasons for all research and inventions. While suffering can be alleviated through the application of scientific discoveries, the Gita teaches that by transcendental experience achieved through the practice of yoga all sufferings are overcome. In fact, it defines yoga as "disconnection from pain". Moreover, one can achieve supreme happiness here in this very world and this very life! This stress on finding salvation on this earth is unique and this positive message runs through all the pages of the Gita. That is why it makes inspiring reading, particularly for those searching to find a purpose in their lives. "You should lift yourself by yourself, for you yourself are your own enemy or best friend", declares Lord Krishna! No teaching can be more positive. There is no room for blaming others for one's failures either in the material or spiritual life – no room for frustration. Life is a challenge and it must be faced discreetly and boldly. We are all responsible beings and as such are accountable for the situations that have been created in the world. The greatest teaching is to "see the whole of creation in yourself and in Me (God)".

The following are a few extracts from the Gita that illustrated how its teachings can be instrumental in establishing a world

Introduction

order in which all beings can live together in harmony and peace. This should be the ultimate aim of man in his march towards building a fair and just world.

When the self is disciplined and the senses restrained, one realizes one's Self as the Self in all beings.

After knowing this, you will not again fall into this confusion. By this you will see the whole of Creation in yourself and in Me.

That yogi is supreme, who judges pleasure or pain everywhere by the same standard he applies to himself.

Knowing Me as the Lord of all Yajnas and asceticism, as the Ruler of all the worlds and the Friend of all beings, he attains peace.

He who is established in oneness, worships Me abiding in all beings. That yogi lives in Me, whatever may be his mode of living.

I am the same to all beings; to Me there is none hateful, none dear. But those who worship Me with devotion, they are in Me and I am also in them.

Even if a man of the most sinful conduct worships Me with undeviating devotion, he must be considered as righteous, for he has made the right resolve.

To those who are ever devout and worship Me with love, I give them the Yoga of Discrimination by which they come to Me.

Out of pure compassion for them, dwelling in their hearts, I destroy the ignorance-born darkness by the luminous Lamp of Wisdom.

When he realizes that the whole variety of beings exists in the One, and is an evolution from that One alone, then he becomes Brahman.

Triple are the gates that lead to hell, destructive of the Self. They are lust, anger and greed. Knowing these three as such, one should therefore reject them.

The man who is liberated from these three gates to damnation, O Kaunteya, practices what is good for him and thus achieves the Supreme Good.

The knowledge by which the one Imperishable Being is seen in all existences, undivided in the divided, know that to be true knowledge (Sattvika).

Because of the lawlessness today, more and more policing and sophisticated instruments are required to cope with the situation. We just can not afford the money spent on jails and armaments which could be used more beneficially. The Gita highlights the source of man's problem and if he can focus his attention seriously in trying to understand and put into practice a little of the principles that are taught, our world can be a different place.

We view the world as a global village but our action is not consistent with that vision. Our minds are still conditioned by the past and as a result we think parochially. We are all living in mental prisons and until we can free the mind from that conditioned state we shall not have harmony and peace. The exclusive attitude and superiority complex that existed will still continue to haunt us. The Gita provides the insights, by which we can expand our vision, enjoy mental peace and live in harmony with the whole of creation.

We are all searching for answers to the problems we are presently facing in the world. They are really on our doorsteps but we are looking far away to find them; just like a man who searches everywhere for his spectacles, when in fact they are on his forehead. It only takes another to point out to him where they are and his problem simply disappears. Similarly, Krishna, the ideal teacher in the Gita, merely brings to our attention how we ourselves create the problems by wrong understanding and how by proper understanding and application they will be resolved; then a peaceful and harmonious atmosphere will prevail. Wars can never be a solution to problems. Understanding is the most sensible answer. And that is what the Bhagavad Gita proposes. Only knowledge can destroy ignorance which is the basic cause of all problems.

THE BHAGAVAD GITA

CHAPTER ONE:

The Yoga Relating to Arjuna's Despondency

1) Translation: Dhritarashtra said: Tell me, O Sanjaya, what my war-like sons and those of Pandu are doing now that they have gathered at Kurukshetra, the field of religious activities?

> *Comment: Although Dhritarashtra is blind, he is still anxious to know about the preparations that are being made for the impending war. He asks his minister, Sanjaya, to inform him about the proceedings. Our attention is drawn to the fact that the war is about to happen in a righteous place (Dharma Kshetra), implying that Dharma (righteousness) is put to the test by adharmic (unrighteous) forces.*

2) Sanjaya said: After looking at the Pandava army arrayed in proper formation, Prince Duryodhana went to his preceptor Drona and said:

3) Behold, O Master, this mighty army of the sons of Pandu which has been arranged into appropriate position by Dhristadyumna, the son of Drupada, your talented disciple.

4) Here are mighty archers, equal in warfare to heroic Arjuna and Bhima, Yuyudhana, Virata, Drupada,

5-6) Dhrishtaketu, Chekitana, and the heroic King of Kasi, Purujit, Kuntibhoja and Saibya, the best among men; and indeed the courageous Yudhamanyu, the brave Uttamauja, Saubhadra and the sons of Draupadi – all of them are great chariot-warriors.

Comment 2-6: Sanjaya related to the King how Duryodhana spoke to Drona about the formation of the Pandavas' army and drew his attention to the great and valiant warriors who were supporting them.

7) Know also, O the best of the twice-born, all those who are our distinguished chiefs, the leaders of my army; I mention them for your information.

8) Your venerable self, Bhishma, Karna, Kripa the victorious in encounter, as well as Asvatthama, Vikarna and the son of Somadatta.

9) There are other heroes also who are well trained in warfare and equipped with manifold weapons and missiles who are ready to lay down their lives for my sake.

10) Multitudinous is our army under the command of Bhishma, but meagre is theirs marshalled by Bhima.

11) Now all of you, position yourselves in your respective divisions and by all means protect Bhishma alone.

Comment 7-11: He then quite cleverly compared his supporters with those of the Pandavas and concluded that his army far outnumbered theirs. The implication is that his army was more powerful and the outcome seemed to be clear in his mind! The protection of Bhishma was important because if he were killed the result could be different! He seems to rely heavily on Bhishma in the impending battle.

12) In order to cheer up Duryodhana, Bhishma the mighty grandsire, the oldest of the Kurus, now roared like a lion and blew his conches.

Comment: Bhishma already knew in whose favour the war would end but gave Duryodhana a false sense of impending victory by challenging the Pandavas.

The Yoga Relating to Arjuna's Despondency

13) Then suddenly there was a terrific noise as conches and kettledrums, tabors, trumpets and cow-horns blared forth.

Comment: The entire army responded in support of Bhishma, making Duryodhana feel confident.

14) Then Madhava and Pandava who were seated in their magnificent chariot yoked to white steeds, gracefully blew their Divine conches.

15) Panchajanya was blown by Hrishikesa, and Devadatta by Dhananjaya. Vrikodara of terrible exploits blew his great conch Paundra;

16) The King Yudhisthira, son of Kunti, blew Anantavijaya; Nakula and Sahadeva blew Sugosha and Manipushpaka.

17) And the Ruler of Kasi, an adept archer and Sikhandi the great chariot-warrior, Dhrhtadyumna and Virata and also Satyaki the invincible;

18) O Ruler of the Earth! Drupada and the sons of Draupadi, and the mighty armed son of Subhadra, all of them blew their own conches as well.

19) Filling the earth and the sky with reverberation, that turbulent sound shook the hearts of the sons of Dhrtarashtra.

Comment 16-19: But the powerful noise from the Pandavas' army was far greater than they expected. At that moment it was expected that all the supporters of both sides had assembled but the Pandavas having a smaller army might have felt vulnerable!

20) Looking at Dhrtarashtra's host positioned and ready to fight, Pandava, whose chariot's flag carries an emblem of Hanuman, lifted his bow and spoke these words to Krishna.

21-22) Arjuna said: Place my chariot, O Achyuta, between the two armies so that I may observe those who are eager to fight that stand here, with whom I must wage this war.

23) I wish to recognize those who gather here to please the evil-minded son of Dhrtarashtra in battle.

> *Comment 20-23: According to tradition, Hanuman did not go to Vaikuntha with his Lord but remained on earth to protect the devotees. At a meeting between him and Arjuna he learnt about the impending war and promised to support him. The emblem on the banner is symbolic of his presence. Arjuna realises that the war has become inevitable and wants to have a good look at those who are supporting him and those supporting the evil Duryodhana.*

24-25) Sanjaya said: After placing the best of chariots between the two armies facing Bhishma and Drona and all the rulers of the earth, Hrishikesa spoke, "O Partha, behold all the Kurus gathered here together."

> *Comment: This is the first time Krishna is speaking in the Bhagavad Gita. As a great Teacher, He did not question Arjuna's decision but simply obliged him. 'All the Kurus' means both sides of the Kuru clan.*

> *Arjuna has an idea of the warriors who would support both sides. But seeing all those who are arrayed on both sides has a great impact on him.*

26) Then Partha saw in both armies paternal uncles, grandfathers, teachers, maternal uncles, cousins, sons, grandsons, comrades, fathers-in-law and benefactors.

27) When the son of Kunti saw those kinsmen in their positions, he was filled with sadness and spoke with heartbreaking compassion.

The Yoga Relating to Arjuna's Despondency

Comment 26-27: Quite naturally he becomes conscious of his loving relations and when he sees some of the most respectable persons in the family involved in the war, this makes him very sad.

28) Arjuna said: O Krishna! Seeing my kinsmen who have gathered here eager to fight, my limbs fail me and my mouth dries up.

29) My body quivers and my hair stands on end. This Gandiva bow slips from my hand and my skin burns all over.

30) I am unable to stand; my head swirls as it were; and O Kesava, I see only adverse omens.

Comment 28-30: He was very disturbed by what he saw. He could clearly see the damage the war would cause. Usually he would fight others without giving it a thought. But this battle is quite different. It involves near and dear ones. That made it very painful. Even if the whole world is seen as one family, this would not prevent wars. Wars are caused by injustices and unfairness that are practised by one against another.

31) I do not think any good can be achieved by slaughtering of kinsmen in battle. O Krishna, I do not crave for victory or empire or even pleasures.

32) What is the good of a kingdom to us or enjoyment or even life, O Govinda?

33) Those for whose enjoyment and pleasures we should seek a kingdom, they stand here in battle, ready to give up their lives and property.

Comment 31-33: Success in the war depends on Arjuna and he is aware of that. But he has taken it very personally and drew his conclusions based on attachment to sound family values. Clearly, one should find happiness in making sacrifices for the benefit of the family – that is the norm. But the dilemma is that the others do not share these values. And Arjuna is confronted with a situation which is difficult to resolve.

34) In both armies Partha saw teachers, fathers, sons as well as grandfathers, maternal uncles, fathers-in-law, grandsons, brothers-in-law and other relatives.

35) I would rather be killed, O Madhusudhana, than try to slay them even for the sake of domination over the three worlds, not to speak of this earth.

Comment 34-35: He is deeply touched when he sees those revered ones with whom he would have to fight. He is mentally prepared to be killed by them rather than fighting them.

36) What delight can we derive, O Janardana, by exterminating these sons of Dhrtarashtra? We shall only commit sin by slaying these villains.

37) We should therefore desist from slaying the sons of Dhrtarashtra, our kinsmen. O Madhava! How can we be happy after killing our own kinsmen?

Comment 36-37: They may be criminals but one thing should be remembered: they are our cousins! Arjuna's conclusion is based on family tradition but he seems to ignore the traditional values that sustain the entire family.

38) Although there are those whose understanding, tainted by greed, see no guilt in exterminating a family or no crime in hostility to friends,

39) Why should we who see evil in the destruction of a family, not desist from such a sin, O Janardana!

Comment 38-39: Those who are ignorant may be excused for committing a wrong. But those who commit it wilfully are really the guilty ones. How true! In the world there have always been good and evil people. But when those who are supposed to be good commit evil deeds, then Dharma is said to be on decline. Because instead of protecting Dharma, they indulge in destroying those values that sustain Dharma. But is that so in this case? Arjuna seems to think that it is.

40) When there is a decline of a family, its time-honoured customs and sacred rites perish, and then immorality overtakes the entire family.

Comment: Heritage consists of traditional customs and sacred rites. With the degeneration of its basic values nothing remains to sustain the society. The sense of sacredness also disappears with it and life becomes a pursuit of pleasure. Society then indulges freely in habits that are contrary to principles that once sustained the family.

41) With the growth of impiety, O Krishna, the family-women become unchaste and when women are corrupted, O Varshneya, social admixture is the result.

Comment: Arjuna stressed that when women, who are the support of the family, become corrupted there is no longer respect for the social laws that once maintained moral conduct in the society.

42) Hell is certainly the lot of the family and the family-destroyers through the disintegration of caste values; for, they are responsible for the fall of their ancestors, being deprived of the cakes and libations offered to them.

43) The everlasting caste-virtues and the family-merits get ruined because of the caste-confusion created by the bad deeds of the family-destroyers.

44) We have heard, O Janardana, that hell is certainly the long lasting abode of the men whose family religious practices have relapsed.

> *Comment 42-44: As a result of the social disorder (caste-confusion) and neglect of family values, the ancestors would suffer because their descendants would loose faith in the rituals related to offerings made to them. It is believed that without receiving those offerings the ancestors will be in everlasting hell. This remembrance of the ancestors helps to maintain social stability.*

45) Because of greed to enjoy the pleasures of a kingdom, we are now about to commit a great sin by killing our kinsmen.

46) If the sons of Dhritarashtra should slay me with the weapons in their hands while I remain unresisting and unarmed in the battle, that would indeed be better for me.

> *Comment 45-46: In conclusion, Arjuna maintained that to fight this war just for the sake of a kingdom would be a grave mistake. If by sacrificing his life that could be avoided, it would be better. He is prepared to lay down his life if that would prevent the war.*

47) Sanjaya said: After uttering those words and being overwhelmed with sorrow in the battlefield, Arjuna sat on the seat of his chariot and lay down his bow and arrows.

> *Comment: Sanjaya continues to narrate to Dhristarashtra what is happening and he must have been happy to know about Arjuna's attitude towards the war. He must have thought that Arjuna's final decision of laying down his arms would mean that the war has ended and his sons would live happily as inheritors of the Kingdom.*

CHAPTER TWO:

THE YOGA OF KNOWLEDGE

1) Sanjaya said: Madhusudhana then spoke these words to him who was thus overwhelmed with compassion and drowned in distress, and whose eyes were filled with tears of despondency.

> *Comment: The suspense is maintained as Sanjaya informs Dhritarashtra that Krishna intervenes when He sees Arjuna's state of mind.*

2) The Blessed Lord said: How is it that this unmanly, heaven-barring and shameful dejection has come upon you, at this critical moment, O Arjuna?

> *Comment: Arjuna is known for his bravery and courage. The Pandavas had suffered immensely at the hands of Duryodhana. All along he was looking forward to the moment when he could avenge the wrong. This sudden change in his attitude gives the impression that he is a coward and out of fear, at the last moment, he has decided not to fight. The word 'anarya' means ignoble, one who lacks courage. It is antithesis to 'arya', a term that signifies those who follow the Path of the great Vedic Dharma – i.e. those who are civilized. And by this is meant those who adhere to the path of truth.*

3) Yield not, O Partha, to such weakness. It is not befitting to a person like you. Get rid of this petty feeble-mindedness and wake up, O vanquisher of foes!

> *Comment: Krishna urges Arjuna to rise above weakness and timidity which are not qualities that befit a warrior who should concentrate on how to achieve victory over the enemies. This pathetic attitude of Arjuna forces Krishna to take control of the situation.*

4) Arjuna said: O slayer of Madhu, O slayer of foes, how shall I counter-attack Bhishma and Drona with arrows who are worthy of worship?

> *Comment: Arjuna's plea is that on the opposite side are people who are worthy of the highest respect and he was thus put in an impossible situation. In this regard he is following what the Dharma teaches and only a truly virtuous person can make such assessment. Others would disregard all ethics and principles and think only in terms of winning the battle and enjoying the booty! The world is full of those kinds of people who have materialistic ambitions and are prepared to disregard all moral principles in order to achieve their objectives. To them, the end justifies the means!*

5) I deem it much better to beg for one's bread than to slay these great-souled masters. If I kill them, my enjoyment of wealth and desires in this world itself will be tainted with blood.

> *Comment: Arjuna's deep concern of what the after-effect would be is worthy of our greatest esteem. It is one thing to fight and win. But how many think about the aftermath! Thinking about that itself may have an impact that can prevent wars. How many think that it is wrong to enjoy at other people's expenses? This is a moral question which needs to be addressed and not pushed under the carpet just because everyone would be found guilty! It is the way forward if conflicts and wars are to be avoided.*

6) I do not know whether it is better for them to conquer us or we conquer them: these very sons of Dhrtarashtra who stand here

before us, after slaying whom we should not care to live.

> *Comment: The war still weighs on his mind. He is not certain whether he is doing the right thing and the anguish is still there – will life be worthy of living after that? The war is no longer an impulsive event. A lot of thinking has passed through Arjuna's mind.*

7) I feel very depressed by not knowing what to do; my understanding is confused regarding my duty. I entreat You, tell me definitely what is good for me. I am Your disciple. Do instruct me who has taken refuge in You.

> *Comment: Arjuna now feels that the problem is beyond him and he needs a second opinion. No one else could fit that position better than Krishna who has been his dear friend. However, in this instance he looks upon him as more than a friend. He addresses him as his Guru and asks him to guide him, being in this state of mental confusion.*

8) Even if I were to gain unrivalled and prosperous monarchy on earth or sovereignty over the celestials, that will not be a remedy to this grief that parches my senses.

9) Sanjaya said: After addressing the Lord of the senses thus, Gudaseka, the terror to the foes, submitted to Govinda, 'I shall not fight,' and kept silent.

> *Comment 8-9: Arjuna saw that no material or celestial gain could compensate for the slaying of those who are so dear to him in the impending war and concludes that he is not going to fight.*

10) Then smiling, as it were, Hrishikesa spoke these words to him who was placed between the two armies in a state of dejection.

> *Comment: Krishna is unruffled by the discouraging words of*

Arjuna who is in a miserable mental condition and quite tactfully speaks to him in a cheerful voice. We have to remember that Arjuna is his friend and as such he is able to speak to him in a friendly tone.

11) The Blessed Lord said: You grieve for those who should not be grieved for, yet what you say is full of wisdom. But the wise grieve neither for the dead nor for the living.

Comment: Krishna agrees with Arjuna's analysis of the problem but disagrees with the way he is acting. The man of wisdom understands the realities of life and looks at their basic causes. A policeman should not discriminate between one who breaks the law and another, simply because one of them is a cousin, a friend or a brother. His duty is to prevent people from breaking the law and in so doing, birth and death are secondary factors. He should carry out his duties and if it is necessary to kill the law-breaker to protect the law, he is not at fault. In the ultimate analysis the law is there to protect everyone and if the law is destroyed by the law-breakers, everyone remains unprotected.

12) There was not a time when I, you, nor any of these ruling princes were not. And there will not be a time when we shall all cease to exist.

Comment: Krishna now discusses it from a different perspective. Birth and death, He says, are natural phenomena. They are inseparable. Death is not the end of one's existence. Life persists after death.

13) As the Indweller experiences childhood, youth and old age in the body, similarly, he also passes on to another body. The serene one is not affected thereby.

Comment: He gives an example of how the body changes as one gets older. There is an eternal law, the Law of Decay.

The Yoga of Knowledge

Everything that is born is subjected to this law. The whole Universe is changing all the time. The man of realization knows that death also is a change when the inner Self moves from one body to another and does not worry about it.

14) It is the contact of the senses with their respective objects that create, O son of Kunti, feelings of heat and cold, pleasure and pain. They are fleeting and momentary. Bear them patiently, O Bharata.

Comment: Most people accept what is pleasing to the senses as good and that which is not pleasing is disliked. But the same thing that is liked at one moment may be disliked at another. Therefore, the senses are not proper instruments to help us to decide what is really good and what is not. When we indulge too much in trying to satisfy the senses, we come to suffering. Pleasure and pain are like two sides of the same coin. One cannot exist without the other. In reality, pleasure is another sort of pain, in that it gives only temporary satisfaction. Therefore, one should not become too disturbed by them.

15) That man, O the best of men, is fit for immortality whom these do not torment, who is balanced in pain and pleasure and who is steadfast.

Comment: Our attitude to birth and death are due to natural conditioning by the senses. Krishna now gives the characteristic of the man who attains to the state of deathlessness as one who detaches himself mentally from the feeling of pleasure and pain. To overcome suffering, one has to learn to detach oneself from the source of suffering. That is the purpose of sadhana (spiritual practice). Elsewhere, Krishna defines yoga as 'disconnection from pain'.

16) That which is unreal has no existence; the real never ceases to be. The truth about both has been realised by the seers.

Comment: To us the things we perceive with our senses are real.

For example: we see something with our eyes and therefore we accept it to be real. If we cannot see something we conclude that it does not exist. We know that we can see things with a telescope which cannot be perceived with the naked eyes. We may therefore conclude from this that the senses have their limitations and as such we should not rely on them without proper consideration. Since that is so, we have to look for another source to find out the truth about what is real and what is unreal. Krishna points out to us that the man of realization is the only source from which one can learn about both!

17) Know That to be verily indestructible by which all this is pervaded. None can cause the destruction of the Absolute.

18) Only these bodies of the Indweller, Who is eternal, indestructible and immeasurable, are said to have an end. Fight therefore, O Bharata.

Comment 17-18: In these two verses Krishna defines Reality as That which dwells in everything, eternal, indestructible and immeasurable. The physical aspects that we perceive with our senses do not fall within those categories. Therefore, we may conclude that they are only relatively real because they depend on something else for their existence and knowing them as such is correct knowledge. Giving them absolute values is the cause of suffering.

19) He who thinks of the Atman as slayer and he who considers It as the slain, both of them are ignorant. It slays not, nor is It slain.

Comment: The Atman being the all-pervasive Self by its very nature is free from activities and since it transcends all elements and is unchangeable, nothing can affect it in any way. Anyone who thinks to the contrary is ignorant.

20) The Atman is neither born nor does It die. It does not come

The Yoga of Knowledge

into being nor cease to exist. It is unborn, eternal, stable and ancient. It is not killed when the body is slain.

21) He who knows the Atman as indestructible, eternal, unborn and changeless, how can he slay, O Partha, or cause another to slay?

> *Comment 20-21: Krishna defines the nature of the Atman in these verses, and concludes that anyone who realises the Atman as such cannot — by the very nature of that experience — be a source of violence, or one who can incite another to commit violence. He is emphasizing the impact of such an experience that brings with it a total transformation. One may cite examples of Ratnakar who became Valmiki who wrote the Ramayana or Sidharta who became the Buddha. They had that experience and became enlightened as a result.*

22) As a man casting off worn-out garments puts on new ones, so the embodied one — after casting off worn-out bodies — enters into others that are new.

> *Comment: As we change the clothes we wear from time to time, similarly the body is like the clothes of the Atman or embodied Self which it changes now and again. This change is what we call death. It is not just like a light that went out. We may draw a similarity between this and the rising and setting of the sun. We perceive how the sun rises and we see it until it sets. But what we are not aware of is that the setting sun has its rising somewhere else immediately. If we are at a particular position on the globe, we can see the sun's setting and rising from the same point. Then we would not be bothered about the sun's rising and setting.*
>
> *A man of knowledge knows that in reality the sun never really sets or rises. The man of realization is in that position from where he can see the reality of birth and death, and so he does not rejoice about birth nor grieve over death because that is only*

applicable to the physical body. Like the sun, the Atman is not affected by the changes that take place.

23) Weapons do not cleave the Atman nor can it be burned by fire, wet by water or dried by the wind.

24) This Self is uncleavable, incombustible and neither wetted nor dried. It is eternal, all-pervading, stable, immovable and everlasting.

25) This Atman is said to be unmanifest, unthinkable and immutable. Therefore, knowing it as such, you should not grieve.

Comment 23-25: Krishna defines here in more detail about the nature of the Atman or Self. The Universe is made up of five elements. They are fire, water, earth, air and ether. Since the Atman is subtler than these elements, It cannot be affected by them. The elements depend on the Atman for their existence and not the Atman on them. In this respect even 'hell fire' is of no consequence.

The Atman is 'unthinkable' means that it is Consciousness. Because of Its Presence we are conscious and can think. When the Atman leaves the body, all thinking processes stop. Being immutable, the Atman cannot be divided. Therefore, the question of how many Atman does not arise. From the same earth so many different forms of living and non-living beings and things are born. Similarly, the Atman is the Source of the whole of Creation. From this knowledge ends grief and not from hearsay. That is why it is said that the science of the Self (Atman) is the highest science. Only from Self-knowledge comes the end of grief.

26) Or, even if you think of this Atman as given to constant births and deaths, you should not grieve, O mighty armed one.

27) As death is certain for those who are born; even so birth is certain for those who are dead. You should not therefore lament over what is inevitable.

Comment: Krishna now looks at death from the materialistic point of view. We all witness what happens with all living beings. We witness birth and we see death occurring. That is only one side of the coin. Krishna is drawing a logical conclusion of what happens after that. Since death is certain for every living being, similarly, birth is certain for those who have died. That is the full equation. Life moves in a cyclic pattern, not in a straight line. We know that births and deaths are occurring all the time, therefore, we should accept them since they are an inevitable part of life. If we grieve over it, that will not prevent it from happening. That is a logical conclusion! But, we emotional beings can not help weeping.

28) Beings are all, O Bharata, unmanifested in their origin, manifested in their mid-state and unmanifested again in their end. What is the point then for anguish?

Comment: Physicists are beginning to grasp the idea of these two aspects of life — the unmanifest and the manifest — a concept that has been established by our Rishis for many thousands of years. Krishna is telling us that all beings emerge from the unmanifest state and again return to the unmanifest state. Knowing that this is a continuous process, Krishna consoles us that we should not grieve. There is a continuation of this pattern, which we call reincarnation.

The physicists refer to these two aspects as the 'implicate' and the 'explicate' and accept that whatever we see here has its origin somewhere else! We cannot logically say that nothing existed before the 'big bang'. That would be unscientific.

29) One beholds the Self as wonderful; another speaks of It as marvellous; another again hears of It as strange; though hearing yet another knows It not at all.

Comment: One person realises the Atman and, after coming back to his normal state of consciousness, thinks how wonderful that experience is. Anyone who does not have that experience but simply hears of It from someone else can not know It. This comes under the category of 'belief' and is an admission that he does not know. According to Acharya Swami PranavanandajiMaharaj, founder of the Bharat Sevashram Sangha, one cannot know the Atman by hearsay or from reading books. Only one who experiences It, can be a reliable source to explain the mystery of Its existence.

30) This, the Indweller in the bodies of all, is ever invulnerable, O Bharata. Therefore you should not grieve for any being.

Comment: After presenting several important facts about life, Krishna in conclusion says: What is the use of worrying over what you do not have any control over! Not to speak of death, but even regarding life some unnecessarily worry over so many ordinary things.

31) Again, looking at the importance of your own duty as well, you should not waver because there is nothing more welcome to a Kshatriya than a righteous war.

Comment: After discussing the problem relating to death, Krishna now draws Arjuna's attention to the point of duty. The function of society has been divided into four categories. One of them relates to law and order – to protect the innocent from the wicked. That is Arjuna's duty and Krishna is urging him to look at his position in the order of social justice. As such he should not hesitate to perform his duty. Moreover, in this particular case it is a blessing in disguise. It is something one should accept joyfully because it is fighting for a great cause (Dharma).

32) Those Kshatriyas should be happy, O Partha, who are engaged in such a battle that comes unsought as an open gateway to heaven.

Comment: Warriors should look at this righteous battle as a blessing because even if killed they will go to the heavenly abode. The implication is that usually battles do not confer such great rewards.

We may cite an example in the Ramayana to explain this further. After abducting Sita, Ravana was taking her in his aerial vehicle. Sita was crying for help. Jatayu, a vulture, heard her wailing cry and went to her rescue. In the encounter Jatayu was fatally wounded. While searching for Sita, Rama found the dying bird. Because Jatayu died fighting for a noble cause, Rama considered him as the holiest of the holy and commended his soul to the highest Abode.

33) But if you will not wage this righteous warfare, then, by ignoring your own duty and honour, you will incur sin.

Comment: Arjuna thought that he would be committing a sinful act by fighting his kinsmen. But Krishna tells him that he is absolutely wrong and it will be sinful if he refuses to fight! Perhaps we should examine the implication of the Law of Karma in this respect. Let us look at it from the point of commission and omission. A man, for example, commits a crime and another sees him. Instead of reporting the crime, he remains quiet. According to the Law of Karma, he is equally guilty because in effect he has condoned the act. The law is there to protect the innocent and by not reporting the crime, the law (Dharma) is being violated. Therefore the rule is: 'Dharma rakshitih rakshitah' (he who protects Dharma is protected by Dharma). It is important to be a good citizen, but it is equally important to see that no one breaks the law, because if there is no law, everyone will remain unprotected. If Arjuna does not fight, he will be guilty of omission and of being an instrument in aiding the law-breakers.

34) People will ever recount your bad reputation, and to the honoured, infamy is surely worse than death.

35) The great chariot-warriors will look at you as one fled from war out of fear; and you who were highly esteemed by them will be lightly held.

36) Your enemies will also slander your strength and speak many awful things about you. Can there be anything more painful than that?

37) If you are slain, heaven will be your reward; victorious you will enjoy this earth. Therefore arise, O son of Kunti, and resolve to fight.

38) Regard pain and pleasure, gain and loss, victory and defeat as the same and engage yourself in the battle. Thus you will incur no sin.

> *Comment 34-38: Krishna says to Arjuna that so far He has been giving reasons for fighting the war based on wisdom. Arjuna must also think about his position in society. He was held in great respect. People admired his skill in archery. They were proud of his valour. All of that will suddenly disappear! He emphasizes that there is no loss in fighting the war, no sin committed and urges him to stand up. One can see the great Teacher coming to the end of His presentation in logical sequence rising to the occasion and concludes with a bang as it were! He is urging Arjuna not to look at the battle in a personal way. He is bound by his duty. In this case it is a noble cause and refraining from it would have a tremendous negative impact on him.*

39) The ideal of Self-knowledge has so far been presented to you. Listen now to the ideal of practice. By following this, O Partha, you will be free from the bonds of karma.

> *Comment: Krishna has already given a rational answer to Arjuna's problem. Now He is going to look at it from a practical point of view. He is always positive and assures Arjuna that by following this approach there will be no negative results!*

The Yoga of Knowledge

40) In this there is no loss of effort. There is no adverse effect. Even a little practice of this Dharma saves one from great fear.

> Comment: What a wonderful Dharma this is! No loss of effort! No adverse effect! No medical science can give assurance that the medicine prescribed will not have side effects! Often it creates more problems. Just by making a little effort to follow the Path of Dharma, great problems can be overcome. It keeps one healthy. The fear syndrome is the basic problem of man. We take medicine in order to prolong life. Fear emerges from the awareness that death is certain. Only if we can overcome the sting of death there will be no fear! And this is what Dharma assures us.

41) To the firm-in-mind, O joy of the Kurus, there is but one decision; many-branched and endless are the decisions of the fickle-minded.

> Comment: One of the characteristics of Dharma is 'dhriti' (firmness of mind). The practice of Dharma brings a calm, balanced and steady mind. Only when the mind is in such condition, can one make proper decisions. But when the mind is in an unbalanced state, one is never sure about anything. Lacking of confidence weakens the willpower of an individual and the mind remains in a state of uncertainty.
>
> The advantage of having a steady mind is enormous. The individual uses up far less energy and so he is always energetic. He does less work but with better results. The fickle-minded person never gets anything right however much he tries and in the process burns up a lot of energy. To him life is always a burden. But the man of steady mind enjoys everything in life. He makes unsuccessful pursuits successful.

42) The unwise who delight in the flowery words disputing about the Vedas say that there is nothing other than this.

Comment: There are those, the unwise ones, who argue about the ritualistic aspects of the Vedas, saying that is all. They close their minds to everything else. But the uniqueness of the Vedic teaching is that it is not dogmatic. It is inclusive of different approaches to realise the Absolute. It encourages one to explore and discover the truth as a result of which blossoms great philosophies. This daring attitude of the Vedic seers to question everything before accepting it is unparalleled elsewhere in ancient history.

43) They are desire-ridden and hold the attainment of heaven as the goal of birth and its activities. Their words are laden with specific rites in pursuit of pleasure and lordship.

44) There is no fixity of mind for those who cling to pleasure and power and whose discrimination has been stolen away.

Comment: Krishna explains that pleasure and power create an imbalance in the mind and as a result our power to discriminate is weakened. Lacking in the power to discriminate creates mental inconsistency. To overcome these two abnormal human tendencies, the Vedas teach us to practise self-control (dama – one of the characteristics of Dharma), to control the pleasure instinct, and compassion (daya) to prevail over the evil inclination of power. But disregarding these higher precepts of the Vedas, there are those who perform specific rites for the sake of enjoying pleasure and power, and do such things that will take them to heaven.

45) The Vedas give an account of the three Gunas. You are to transcend the three Gunas, O Arjuna. Be free from the pairs of opposites, even-minded, unconcerned with getting and keeping, and be centred in the Self.

Comment: The three Gunas (primal qualities) in Hindu philosophy occupy a similar position to atoms in physics. They occupy basic positions in both. Krishna will be dealing with

The Yoga of Knowledge

these specifically in another chapter, as they are very intricately involved in the whole discussion. We may assume that Arjuna is aware of their traditional significance and Krishna is advising him here to rise above them and focus his mind on the Self (Atman). To be able to achieve that, we have to be indifferent to the sense of personal possessions, and be free from discrimination. This sense of possession and position create a barrier to inner progress and result in much of the grievances we find in society. In its truest sense, Dharma teaches us not to hoard but to share our possessions with those in need.

46) To an enlightened Brahmana all the scriptures are as useful as a tank when there is a flood everywhere.

Comment: This solitary declaration in this verse puts the Bhagavad Gita above all other scriptures in the world. Here, Krishna is urging us to go above the Book! Do not cling to the Book! And this includes the Bhagavad Gita itself! This does not mean that the scriptures are not useful. Their objective is to elevate us, to take us step by step until we reach where we need to go! The goal is enlightenment. Those who still hold on to the Book are yet in a state of ignorance.

We may use a crude example to explain this further. When we are in a dark cave a torch is very useful. But when we are out of the cave, in broad day light, what is the use of it? We simply put it away!

Our attention is drawn here to the ritualistic part of the Vedas (Karma Kanda). The performer of rituals does so with the expectation of a reward — mostly for the enjoyment of pleasure in this world, or even after death in another world, and power to control and dominate over others.

47) Perform your duty but do not lay claim to its fruits. You should not be the producer of the fruits of karma nor should you lean towards inaction.

Comment: This is one of the most often quoted verses of the Gita and it has a profound psychological significance. It is quite natural for one to expect reward for what he is doing. This is the basis on which the whole world operates. Yet Krishna is telling us that this is not good!

Manu agrees that even the Vedas are studied for the same purpose! Since people are motivated by rewards he says, "To act solely from a desire for reward is not laudable, yet an exemption from that desire is not (to be found) in this (world); for on that desire is grounded the study of the Veda and the performance of actions, prescribed by the Veda".

By not working for reward one achieves the highest, i.e. peace of mind and happiness. After all, that is the basic objective for which we work but we lose sight of it and what we get is a restless mind. It is the expectation of results that causes anxiety and stress. Because in a world of changes there is always uncertainty of what would happen next.

Our success is measured merely by our objective achievement. But there is another side to it and that is equally — if not even more — important. It is the subjective aspect: the impact it has on our mind. We always think that we can escape from that, but it keeps on building up in our nature and ultimately it explodes, because we can no longer contain it. This is the cause of so many mental and physical problems. To be detached from the fruit of action is the means by which we can control our stress problems.

Because reward is the driving force, many people use this verse as an excuse to escape from responsibility. After retirement, a director of a company may go and do a sweeping job in an ashram. He thinks that doing a menial job is a great thing and he tries to impress others that he once occupied a high position! Even material things are easier to renounce than the ego.

Arjuna also wanted to relinquish his duties and live on alms. Krishna ridiculed him for that. We all suffer from the same syndrome even though we may be followers of religion. That is because we do not understand the intricacy of action.

Since reward is the motivating factor of action, we make a distinction between that for which we get more or less incentive. We are naturally inclined to accept that by which we can earn more. We also judge a job as difficult or easy in accordance with its remuneration. Our likes and dislikes are also estimated in the same way. We do not make a distinction between what we like and what is good. We unconsciously decide in favour of what we like! We rarely think in terms of the greatest good.

On the basis of reward there are so many industrial strikes, so much violence, destruction and inactivity. Yet there is hardly any serious study about the subject! Here is where Krishna excels but how many of us try to follow and benefit from it. Like Arjuna, we are all looking for soft options – a comfortable life or a comfortable religion.

That is why Krishna gives a warning: Do not let this indifference to the fruit of action make you inactive! Whatever we are doing, we must put our full heart in it. No work is too high or too low. Only when we apply reward to the work, then its attributes change.

One of the definitions of yoga is skillfulness in action. The implication is that even though one may not look for the fruit of action, still, one should not become indifferent, lethargic and irresponsible.

48) Being fixed in yoga, perform action without attachment, O Dhananjaya, and be even-minded in success and failure. Mental equilibrium is verily what is called yoga.

Comment: Yoga is introduced and one of its definitions is given as mental stability which is attained by maintaining a balanced mind in favourable and unfavourable circumstances. This practice helps to develop awareness of what is happening and enables us to adjust ourselves mentally to meet both with a detached mind. This practice helps to relieve us from a lot of anxieties and stress which keep the mind in a restless state.

49) Motivated karma, O Dhananjaya, is far inferior to that performed with equanimity of mind; take refuge in even-mindedness; wretched are those who seek for the result.

Comment: Krishna emphasises the greatness of that action which is done with a detached mind because it brings happiness and does not create negative reaction. Hence, it produces a harmonious atmosphere which benefits everyone. That is basically the object of yoga. It has both individual and collective advantages.

If action that is motivated by expectation of reward had positive effects, then our world would be a wonderful place. But when each one eyes the cake instead of working for it, much energy is wasted and most often there is calculation of how to get it without doing anything! This calculating attitude is common in human nature.

There is an old story about a King whose birthday was the following day. There was an announcement that the King would like all the subjects to put a pint of milk in a huge vessel during the night. The next morning when the King went and opened the tap to get milk, only pure water was flowing. He was amazed. Everyone thought that if he should put a pint of water instead of milk in the vessel, there could be no chance of the King knowing! Ultimately, there was only water in the tank!

When reward is considered as the primary objective in one's pursuit and the means secondary, moral principles and ethical values that are the pillars upon which trust is built become worthless. This is one of the basic causes of the degeneration of society. Eventually no one trusts the other.

50) One whose mind is established in equanimity is freed in this very life from vice and virtue. Therefore devote yourself to yoga. Work that is done to perfection is really yoga.

> *Comment: Krishna gives another definition of yoga. He emphasises the value of right action. Another form of meditation is to put one's whole heart into what one is doing. Half-heartedness does not take one anywhere. The benefit is that the mind becomes stable and one is liberated from the conditioned state. Initially, the distinction between good and evil is a necessary guide to elevate oneself. But ultimately one becomes free from both. It is like using one thorn to take out another; then both are thrown away. So long as there is attachment, the mind is swayed like a pendulum between the polarities of good and evil which haunts the mind all the time and keeps it busy.*
>
> *If everyone is dedicated to his duty, that is the surest way to build trust. Where there is trust there is no anxiety.*

51) The wise, imbued with evenness of mind, renouncing the fruits of their actions and freed from the fetters of births, verily go to the pure state.

> *Comment: It is because of ignorance that we evaluate an act on the basis of how much we will be rewarded and as a result our mind becomes tainted. But Self-knowledge makes us aware of the negative effect it has, and so we avoid that attitude and enjoy the peace it brings and ultimate liberation which is the purpose of life.*

52) When your understanding transcends the taint of delusion, then shall you gain indifference to things heard and those yet to be heard.

Comment: By practising through the guidance of the Guru one reaches a state of certainty of mind. At that level one is not affected by disputations of others – just like an elephant taking no notice of barking dogs.

53) When your intellect, tossed about by the conflict of opinions, has become poised and firmly fixed in equilibrium, then you shall get into yoga.

Comment: As one progresses in Self-knowledge all confusions and doubts disappear, a state of perfect mental balance is attained and one experiences the unity of existence. This is referred to elsewhere as 'seeing oneself in all beings and all beings in oneself'. That is the yogic state. Reaching that state, all conflicts end. There is no more confusion.

54) Arjuna said: By what sign, O Kesava, a man is to be known, who is steadfast in wisdom and absorbed in Samadhi? How does the man firm in wisdom speak? How does he sit? How does he walk?

Comment: Arjuna has asked a very pertinent question. A person may say: 'I have seen God', but his behaviour and attitude may not be any better than the ordinary man. If there is no difference between the realiser of God and the ignorant man, then what is its worth? This question has been raised in the Vedantasara thus: if the realiser of Brahman eats the same thing as a dog, then what is the difference between him and a dog?

There must be a transformation. He should be like the sun, not requiring an introduction-card or someone to point him out. His attitude and behaviour must reflect what he really is. Yes, Arjuna, being a warrior, is asking practical questions! What are the indications of him who is perfected in yoga? How shall we know him? Are there ways by which we can recognise him?

These are questions that are relevant to the Guru as well. The word means 'he who gets rid of ignorance'. He also should set an example. But if he himself is ignorant, how can he get rid of the ignorance of another? A person's behaviour and attitude reflect what he really is and not what he claims to be. Hinduism emphasises conduct (karma), not beliefs. What a person's conduct is, that is what he is.

55) The Blessed Lord said: O Partha! When a man, free from all the desires of the heart and his lower self, finds satisfaction in the higher Self, then is he said to be one of stable wisdom.

Comment: Only he reaches the state of Samadhi whose heart is empty of all cravings for material things. Desire creates mental instability. Therefore, only when our mental faculties find delight in supernal experience, is the mind at peace, and in peace there is stability.

56) He whose mind is not perturbed by hardship, who does not crave for happiness, who is free from affection, fear and anger, is to be known as the Muni of constant wisdom.

Comment: One should live in the world without being attached to it. Attachment creates an imbalanced attitude that distorts our vision of things. There are different kinds of metal. To be tied by a golden chain is the same as being tied by an iron chain. Attachment to happiness is also a form of bondage. From attachment result fear and anger, which create mental instability and cause a person to behave abnormally.

57) He is poised in wisdom who is unattached everywhere and is not delighted at receiving something good or dejected when some evil comes.

Comment: One should live in the world without being influenced by the pairs of opposites which are the very foundation of the world. To look at them calmly is the means to maintain a peaceful and sober attitude of mind.

58) Just like a tortoise that withdraws its limbs, when a person can withdraw his senses from the sense-objects, then his wisdom is set firm.

> *Comment: After explaining to Arjuna the characteristics of a person who has attained Samadhi, Krishna assumes that the subject-matter he was discussing was not too easy to understand. To simplify it he uses a turtle as an example. He chooses a beautiful example to explain what non-attachment means. It is to turn the extroverted senses inward like the tortoise that withdraws its limbs within.*

59) The man who is abstinent is detached from sense-objects though his longing for them still remains. His longing also ceases when he realises the Supreme.

> *Comment: Krishna teaches us how to accomplish that through the practice of self-restraint. This is what we call self-culture. By practising this, a person achieves physical control over himself. The other part is to have such mental control that there is not even a tinge of desire. Samadhi is attained when there is no more desire and therefore nothing more to relish in this material world.*
>
> *This is an enlightened state when one's vision of the world undergoes a transformation. We have such examples in Maharshi Valmiki and the Buddha. What is important to remember is that the problems of life are not only demonstrated, but solutions to them are offered. The only requirement is the willingness of the victim to apply the principles i.e. to try and help himself.*

60) The excited senses, O son of Kunti, can easily carry away the mind of even a wise man who is striving for perfection.

> *Comment: Here is a warning that when the agitated senses can even have power over the wise man, what chance does*

the ordinary man have over their impact? Therefore, knowing the power of the senses, one should always be aware of the subtle ways in which they can distract an aspirant. And after knowing of their power, an aspirant must always be vigilant.

61) The yogi who has controlled them all, sits and focuses on Me as the Supreme Goal. His wisdom is stable whose senses are under control.

Comment: Finally, Krishna says that He is to be regarded as the ultimate Goal of life. There are other goals which have their values but these are all relative. One must focus on the Goal to be achieved in life, otherwise one is carried away by various diversions and the Goal is never reached.

In these verses (55-61) the emphasis has been on the value of stable wisdom which is only accomplished by those who have control over their senses.

62) Constantly thinking on the objects of senses, man develops attachment to them; from attachment comes desire; from unfulfilled desire comes anger.

63) From anger proceeds delusion; from delusion, confused memory; from confused memory the ruin of reason; when the reason is ruined he perishes.

64) But the disciplined yogi, moving among objects with the senses under control and free from attraction and aversion, gains in tranquillity.

65) In peace all his sorrows are destroyed. For the intellect of the peaceful is soon established in equilibrium.

Comment 62-65: Krishna makes an insightful analysis of man's psychological problems. Earlier he tells us that it is important to have a controlled mind which is achieved through the practice of self-restraint. Here he says that the lacking of self-restraint is the root-cause of all the problems. Because self-indulgence leads to attachment and the consequences of this He masterly presents in a logical order. He shows how it leads to our destruction.

An example of this is a man who first takes one cigarette and then another. Ultimately, he cannot do without it in spite of the doctor's warning of how it is affecting his lungs. This is also true of people who drink alcohol. Attachment is the basic cause of all suffering.

The value of practicing self-control is that peace of mind is attained which is the end of all unhappiness!

66) There is no wisdom in the fickle-minded, nor can he meditate. To the unmeditative, there is no such thing as peace. And how can there be happiness when there is no peace?

Comment: With a restless mind one cannot think properly or sit still for a moment. And without being able to sit quietly and focus the mind, one cannot experience peace. Only when the mind is at rest can we experience peace. Since the source of happiness is peace, one can never be happy with a mind that is in a restless state.

Yet, we accept pleasure as happiness although pleasure and pain are two sides of the same coin. Wherever there is pleasure, there is also pain. When we are ignorant of anything better than pleasure, we surrender to it like an animal that is taken to a slaughterhouse!

67) Just as a gale carries away a ship on the waters, similarly the mind that yields to the roving senses takes away a man's power of discrimination.

The Yoga of Knowledge

Comment: Krishna again gives an example of what happens when the mind is not controlled so that we can fully understand the power of the senses upon it. The faculty of dispassion (intellect) differentiates man from lower forms of life. When that is affected, he becomes more dangerous than an animal, because his capacity for destruction is immense, and ultimately that leads to self-destruction.

68) Therefore, O mighty-armed, his cognition is well poised whose senses are completely restrained from their objects.

Comment: The conclusion is that it is to our greatest advantage and well-being that we should make an effort to have control over the senses so that our insight to things will be clearer. And one will become one's natural self.

69) That which is night to all beings, that is the time when the disciplined man is awake; that time in which all beings are awake, is night to the Atman-cognizing Muni.

Comment: Krishna is saying that the things that normally attract the ordinary man, the aspirant abstains from. And the aspirant who practises abstention likes the things that are repulsive to the ordinary man. It is a matter of choice between the pleasant and the good. The pleasure in which a worldly man indulges, the aspirant practises self-restraint.

70) Not he who is full of desires attains peace, but the man in whom all desires have merged like the rivers which flow into the ocean that is full and unmoving.

Comment: From attachment comes desire. Unfulfilled desire is the cause of suffering. When there is no more desire to be fulfilled, one attains to the peaceful state.

71) That man attains peace who lives without longing, freed from all desires and the feeling of 'I' and 'mine'.

Comment: Earlier, Krishna has been discussing the effects of attachment, longing and desire. Now He has added two characteristics that have bad effects on our life. They are the ego and the sense of possession and He leaves them at that for the moment.

72) This, O Partha, is the Brahman state. After attaining this, there is no more confusion. Being established in it even at the moment of death, a man gets into oneness with Brahman.

Comment: Krishna defines the Absolute as a state that is free from all contradictions. To reach that state is the purpose of life and the advantage is that it can be attained here and now! And after attaining It, one can enjoy heavenly bliss even in this earthly body. Here is an encouragement to try to make an effort.

This chapter ends with two alluring verses relating to the nature of Brahman, the ego and personal possession. In conclusion we may add that there has been a great emphasis on the value of peace and how it can be achieved through self-culture and not by self-indulgence.

CHAPTER THREE

THE YOGA OF ACTION

1) Arjuna said: O Janardana! If You think that knowledge is superior to action, then, O Kesava, why are You forcing me into this terrible battle?

Comment: Arjuna now intervenes with something that was bothering his mind. He was listening carefully to what Krishna was saying and the subject-matter was pleasing to him. Yet, he does not understand why he has to be involved in fighting. He speaks frankly to Krishna: if what You say is correct, then why are You forcing me to engage in this fratricidal war?

2) With these perplexing words, You are, as it were, confusing my understanding. Tell me definitely that path which I may follow and attain the Supreme.

Comment: Arjuna is saying to Krishna as it were: at first You were forcing me to fight this battle as a way to salvation which I did not like anyway. Then You so highly commend this alternative, which is so attractive: no fighting, free from attachment, desire and longing, no responsibility, no duty, etc. I do not understand why You are forcing me to follow that difficult path of fighting a battle.

He appeals to Krishna to tell with certainty that which is best for him.

3) The Blessed Lord said: O sinless one! This twofold path was

given by Me to the world at the beginning of Creation. The Path of Knowledge has been given to those who are intellectually inclined and the Path of Work to those who are active.

> *Comment: Evolution takes place along two lines – observation and experience. Some learn by seeing what has caused pain to others and try to avoid that thing. Others, who are not so clever, get burnt in order to learn. These are the two natural ways which beings follow from the very beginning of Creation. One is active, the other is passive. In time, each has been developed for a higher purpose in accordance with the natural tendencies. This insightful application is known as yoga. Both integrate at a higher level of evolution.*

4) Man does not attain to the state of actionlessness simply by abstaining from activity, nor does he rise to perfection by mere renunciation.

> *Comment: 'Actionless' here means 'mental poise'. This state of mind is not achieved just by abstaining from physical activities and by merely renouncing the performance of rituals is not an indication that one has attained a state of perfection. It has been explained earlier what the signs of a realised Soul are.*

5) None can really remain actionless even for a moment. Indeed, everyone is helplessly driven to action by his own nature, born of Prakriti.

> *Comment: Everyone behaves according to what his nature is. Prakriti is made up of three Gunas which are its primal qualities and these Gunas are inherent in the whole of Creation. As mentioned earlier, Krishna will discuss this in a special chapter because it needs to be dealt with on its own. It is enough at this point for us to understand that we are under the control of our nature.*

6) That deluded man is called a hypocrite who sits and controls

the organs of action, but allows his mind to muse on the objects of the senses.

> *Comment: Here is a question of longing for something but restraining oneself from actually enjoying that thing. It is important to remember that karmic fruits are not related only to what we do but what we think of as well. Therefore, to cogitate over something is almost as good as participating in that act. A hypocrite is someone who pretends to be one thing but in reality he is something else. Krishna condemns this deceitful attitude. This deceitfulness is often practised in the name of religion.*

7) But he excels, O Arjuna, who restrains his senses by the mind, is unattached, and engages his organs of action on the Path of Activity.

> *Comment: The recommendation is to control the senses and apply the relevant organs in what is required to be done. We have seen that the body is only an instrument that follows the dictates of the senses. It functions for the good of all when the mind is free from the influences of the senses which operate on the basis of instincts.*

8) Engage yourself in doing works that are compulsory, for action is indeed superior to inaction. By being inactive the mere maintenance of the body will not be possible.

9) The whole world is bound by actions except those that are performed for the sake of Yajna. Therefore, O son of Kunti, diligently perform action for Yajna alone, free from attachment.

> *Comment 8-9: Everyone works with a selfish motive and as a result lives in bondage. Krishna urges us to work with a heart full of sacrifice and enjoy the spirit of freedom. It is attachment that keeps the world in this chaotic condition. Excepting those acts that are performed with altruistic attitude*

every other act leads to bondage. The way to free oneself from this mental prison is to perform selfless activities.

10) After creating mankind in the beginning together with Yajna, Prajapati the Creator said: "By this shall you propagate. Let this be the milch cow by which your desires find fulfilment".

Comment: From the very beginning of Creation mankind has been warned not to become selfish but to find enjoyment by following the principle of Yajna. However, in time it was forgotten and that was the beginning of suffering.

There is a story in one of the Upanishads that when the suffering in the world was unbearable, the leader of the gods, demons, and man went to the Creator to ask His advice. To each of them He said, "Da". When they returned to their respective community, they mentioned what Prajapati had said. As the community of the gods pondered over what has been said, one of the wise ones said: "We gods are ever youthful. We do not suffer from diseases. Our problem is that we do not know how to overcome our passion." By 'da' the Grandfather meant 'daman'. We must practise self-control, then we will overcome the cause of our suffering.

The leader of the demons also returned to his community and they also deliberated on the meaning of the word. A wise one among them said: we are very powerful and strong and are not afraid of anyone. We have become egoistic and domineering. The Creator meant by 'da' that we should practise 'daya'. We must be compassionate, only then we shall enjoy peace of mind.

When the representative of man returned, he also related what Prajapati had said. At first they could not understand what the Creator meant but a wise one got the answer. Humans are by nature greedy and want to hoard everything. By 'da' the Grandfather meant 'dana'. If we want to experience peace we must be charitable. We must share what we have with others. 'Da da da' is known as the voice of the thunder and explains briefly how one can have peace in a world full of strife. Youth without self-control is wasting of energy. Power without compassion is tyranny. And wealth without the spirit of sharing is poverty.

In this very important verse, Krishna tells us that by following the principle of self-denial the whole world will be happy. In the first verse of the Isa Upanishad there is a caution: Knowing fully well that everything belongs to the Supreme, take only that much as you need.

11) Be grateful to the Devas for this; and may those Devas cherish you. Thus by relishing what is given by one another, you shall reap the supreme good.

Comment: There must be mutual self-giving. Someone has given you something; express a sense of gratitude for that and when the need arises, you should also offer something to him. In this way everyone will be benefited and there is no greater good than that! When we try to enjoy at the expense of others, we are unwittingly creating a negative reaction which will sooner or later explode.

12) "When cherished by the Yajna, the Devas shall reward you with the enjoyments you desire." A thief verily is he who enjoys what they give without giving anything to them in return.

Comment: Yajna here means the making of offerings into the sacred Fire. According to the sacred texts these offerings are meant for the guardian deities who encompass our solar system. Our livelihood depends on the regular appearances of the seasons which are maintained through the principle of nourishing and not exploitation of nature.

When we apply the same principle to our social order, it means we should not only take from society but must contribute as well. Krishna again uses very harsh words for those who take without making any contribution. Such persons are bandits. They have no place in a civilized society. They must be kept behind bars, because such parasites drain the world of its richness and are the causes of poverty.

13) The virtuous ones who eat the remnants of Yajna are freed from all sins; but the sinful ones who cook food only for their own satisfaction, they verily eat sin.

Comment: Those who share their possessions with others are the virtuous ones, but those who only think of themselves, of their own enjoyment and happiness, are living in sin.

14) From food beings are born; from rain food is produced; rain comes from Yajna; Yajna originates from karma.

Comment: There is a cyclic pattern, a series of interdependencies through which life maintains its existence. Without food nothing can live. Crops depend on the rains. The rain comes when there are clouds in the sky. The clouds are formed from the smoke that emanates from the sacred Fire and this requires the performance of rituals in which offerings are made. Thus, a natural process is maintained.

15) Know karma to have originated from the Veda, and the Veda from the Imperishable. The all-pervading Veda is, therefore, ever-present in Yajna.

Comment: The method of ritualistic performance is directed by the sacred text. This revealed text has a direct connection with the Imperishable. Therefore, the Imperishable in the form of the sacred text exists in acts of performances of sacrifice. As such, all sacrificial acts are considered as divine.

16) He who does not follow here on earth this wheel thus revolving, sinful in living and rejoicing in the senses, such a person, O Partha, lives in vain.

Comment: From verse nine of this chapter, Krishna explains some of the basic components of Hindu social philosophy. Life is interdependent and therefore it is to the advantage of everyone to look after the interest of the other. That is the least he should do to maintain the orderly functioning of society. And if a person does not follow this Dharma Chakra (Wheel of Life) then his life as a human being has no value.

17) But only for that man who rejoices in the Self, is satisfied with the Self, and is centred in the Self, there verily is no obligatory duty.

Comment: By following the Chakra (Rotating Wheel) of obligatory duties, one evolves to a position when duties are transcended. So long as one depends on another, he has an obligation. That obligation ends only when his whole being is absorbed in the Atman or pure Self.

18) Because there is no object in this world for him to acquire by performing action, nor is there any loss by not doing any action and he does not depend on anyone for anything.

Comment: Krishna explains why that is so. Because his purpose of life has been fulfilled by the contribution he has made, he no longer has any need, so he is independent.

19) Therefore, engage in your obligatory duty without attachment. By doing duty without attachment man verily obtains the Supreme.

Comment: Krishna emphasizes the importance of duty in the scheme of life. When duties are done without self-interest, one realises the Supreme Being. Therefore, one should not neglect one's duty or think that they are not part of the spiritual process. Krishna is saying that it is the most important part because it is the foundation on which society rests. If everyone pursues his own self-interest, there will be no stability in society and the whole world will suffer.

20) Janaka and others indeed achieved perfection by the performance of action; also bearing in mind the need to guide ordinary men, you should perform action.
21) Whatever a great man does, that is followed by others; people go by the example he sets.

> *Comment 20-21: In case there is any doubt, here is an example of a King, Janaka, who indeed attained perfection by performing his duties. It is particularly important that a great man should set a good example, because it is a known fact that the common man always tries to emulate the great.*

22) There is nothing in the three worlds, O Partha, that has not been done by Me, nor anything attained that might be attained; still I engage in action.

23) If ever I did not engage in work ceaselessly, O Partha, men would in every respect follow My Path.

24) These worlds would perish if I did not perform action and I should be the cause of confusion of species and destruction of these beings.

> *Comment 22-24: Not to speak of great men, Krishna is offering Himself as an example. Here God Himself is setting the example of being bound by duties! For the ordinary man duty ends when he no longer depends on anyone. Krishna does not depend on anyone but He still performs action by setting an example. Otherwise, if He did not, others would do the same and there will be disorder, causing everything to perish.*

> *This is also of relevance to our concept of the nature of God Whom we worship and the example saintly people set by their attitude and behaviour. If we are to characterize God,*

> *He should be beyond the negative qualities that are the sources of conflict: God should not hate or be jealous of anyone; He should not exude fear, and He should not be the source of any negative qualities – otherwise He is setting a poor example for the worshippers and the world will be in chaos.*

25) As the unenlightened act from attachment to action, O Bharata, the enlightened also should act but without attachment and with the desire of guiding the multitude.

26) Let not the wise man confuse the mind of ignorant people attached to karma. By performing action persistently and properly, let the wise induce the others in all activities.

> *Comment 25-26: Krishna is warning us that people's understanding is at different levels and therefore it is necessary to be cautious when dealing with society. Rather than too much talking, setting a good example is more effective. Most people are good at talking but bad at setting the right example. That is how society becomes confused and breaks down.*

27) The Gunas of Prakriti perform all karma. But with the understanding clouded by egoism, man thinks: "I am the doer."

28) But, O mighty-armed, the one who is aware of the nature of Guna and Karma knows that Gunas as senses merely abide with Gunas as objects, and he does not become entangled.

29) Those who are deluded by the Gunas of Prakriti get attached to the functions of the Gunas. The man of perfect knowledge should not unsettle the minds of ordinary people whose knowledge is imperfect.

> *Comment 27-29: Here is a hint about the nature and function of the Gunas. In reality the Gunas are the sources of action, but we think that we are acting as independent*

agents. This is because we are blinded by our ego. There is a connection between each sense organ and a sense object, and that attracts the sense. For example, wind is the object of the sense of touch. In this way there is a spontaneous reaction between them. But when we become aware of this, then we are able to dissociate ourselves from the effect. Those who do not understand this, become attached to action, but those with better understanding must not look down upon them but try to guide them.

30) Surrendering all actions to Me, with your thoughts resting on the Self, freed from hope and selfishness, and cured of mental fever, engage in battle.

Comment: This message to Arjuna is applicable to all of us. With the teachings that have been given one must have reached a point when one is convinced about what Krishna is saying. Therefore, one should submit oneself to Him and engage in the performance of one's duty. By so doing, every act becomes a form of worship and a closer relationship is developed with the Lord that brings peace and happiness.

31) Those who always accept this teaching of Mine, full of inner conviction and free from quibbling, they too are released from the bondage of actions.

Comment: Just by accepting this teaching that is related to the performance of duty with faith, one will experience mental freedom and peace.

32) But those who find fault with My teaching and do not put it into practice, deluded as they are in all knowledge and devoid of discrimination, know them to be ruined.

Comment: But those who reject this principle as it is set forth without proper reasoning, they in their ignorance are destroying themselves by not experiencing mental peace.

33) Even a wise man behaves in conformity with his own nature. All beings behave according to their nature; what purpose shall restraint serve?

> *Comment: A man's second self is his nature. What his nature is, that is what he is. Our whole attitude and behaviour are in conformity with our nature. Since that is so, unless mental restraint is followed by practical application to purify the natural instincts, it does not serve its purpose.*

34) Attachment and aversion of the senses for their respective objects are natural. None should come under their domination. They are verily his enemies.

> *Comment: It is a fact of life that we have our likes and dislikes. The same thing we like at one moment we may dislike at another. These 'likes' and 'dislikes' are due to the play of the senses and we should not allow them to dictate to us. We should adhere to higher principles in spite of the enticement of the senses. Otherwise, they will lead us astray like an enemy.*

35) One's own Dharma, though defective, is still better than the Dharma of another well discharged. It is better to die in one's own Dharma; the Dharma of another is full of fear.

> *Comment: This is another of the most often quoted verses of the Gita. It has relevance to caste-duties. These duties are related to the strata in which one is placed in society. Sometimes it is argued that one should not be bound by the social rules. There should be freedom of choice. But Krishna is saying that one should remain at one's position and carry out whatever duties that entails rather than seeking the opportunity that is available beyond one's present social position. Because, one may assume, that will come under the category of 'likes' and 'dislikes' which are personal. That leads to attachment. Performance of obligatory duty is based on an impersonal principle where the welfare of all is the primary*

> *objective. Therefore, although it may appear to be personally unsatisfactory, it is better to stick to it. There is always the uncertainty of finding full satisfaction in any vocation.*

36) Arjuna said: But what is it that forces a man to commit sin unwillingly, O Varshneya, as if he is inhibited by another power?

> *Comment: Arjuna poses an eternal question. What causes us to do wrong things in spite of knowing what is right? It appears as if there is another agent that forces us against our will. This universal question has been answered differently by different religions. Unless we understand this we are living in a hopeless situation. Because, firstly one should know the enemy, and secondly how to conquer it. If the enemy is invisible, there is little chance of overcoming it.*

37) The Blessed Lord said: It is desire, it is wrath begotten by the Rajo-Guna. It is full of passion and all-sinful. Know this as the real enemy here on Earth.

> *Comment: Krishna points directly to the problem, shows its basis and how it operates. This thing called 'desire' is man's number one enemy. Everyone thinks that his enemy is an external foe. But Krishna is pointing to its position within. It is part of our own nature!*

38) As fire is covered by smoke, as mirror by dust and an embryo by the womb, so is this covered by that.

39) Knowledge is covered, O son of Kunti, by this insatiable fire of desire which is the constant foe of the wise.

> *Comment 38-39: This is another example to explain a very subtle subject. When the mirror is full of dust we cannot see our image in it. This does not mean that the substance does not exist. When we clean the mirror, the image is clearly seen. Similarly, this desire exists as a result of ignorance but when*

the light of knowledge reveals itself like the sunshine, the darkness of ignorance which the man always guards himself against disappears.

40) The senses, the mind and the intellect are said to be the source from where it deludes man by veiling his wisdom.

41) Therefore, O eminent of the Bharatas, first control the senses, then slay this sinful destroyer of knowledge and realisation.

Comment 40-41: The organs of the senses, the mind the intellect are the sources through which the enemy operates by inciting the passions and as a result man behaves abnormally. Therefore one should concentrate on controlling the senses which, like the dust that covers the mirror, is like a thick cloud that hides the sunlight of knowledge and deludes us into thinking that it is night.

42) The senses are said to be superior to the body; the mind is superior to the senses; the intellect superior to the mind; and what is superior to the intellect is Atman.

43) Thus knowing Him as superior to the intellect, restrain the self by the Self, O mighty-armed, and slay the enemy in the form of desire, difficult to overcome.

Comment 42-43: Here is a systematic arrangement in order of superiority by which the organs have been presented and after understanding their positions, and that one which is most powerful to them all, this enemy – in the form of desire – which operates through the sense organs, must be overcome by subordinating it to the power of the Self through the practice of meditation.

CHAPTER FOUR:

The Yoga of Renunciation of Action in Knowledge

1) The Blessed Lord said: This imperishable Yoga, I declared to Vivasvat; Vivasvat taught it to Manu and Manu told it to Ikshvaku.

2) Being transmitted in regular succession, the royal-sages knew it. But after a very long time there was a decay of this Yoga in this world, O scorcher of foes.

3) The same ancient Yoga has been taught to you today by Me, for you are My devotee and friend; and this secret is supreme indeed.

> *Comment 1-3: Krishna is now introducing yoga proper by telling Arjuna in the same way as He gave the twofold paths at the very beginning of Creation, similarly He had taught yoga to the very first Manu, Vivasvat, in the beginning of the first cycle of Creation. That knowledge of yoga, which is eternal, was handed successively to the descendants of Vivasvat. We are to understand that this knowledge was only known to the Kshatriya clan and after a time it declined.*
>
> *He confided to Arjuna that it was the same knowledge He was going to teach him. Why does Krishna choose Arjuna of all other great people? Because, although there are many great men and Krishna has a very good relationship with them all, His relationship with Arjuna is very special. He may love and respect others for various reasons. But Arjuna is a genuine devotee and as such He has a special love for him. He must*

The Yoga of Renunciation of Action in Knowledge

talk to him gently and Arjuna must talk to Him with veneration. Between friends there is openness and this is what characterizes the discussion between the two of them.

This is very relevant to our times. Dialogues cannot be successful unless they are done with the spirit of friendship. Solutions can only be achieved when everyone involved has a friendly attitude towards one another. When there is distrust and suspicion and each one tries to score a point, dialogue is never successful.

4) Arjuna said: Later was Your birth and earlier was the birth of Vivasvat. How then am I to understand that You told it to him in the beginning?

Comment: Arjuna raises an objection. He wants to know how is it possible for Krishna to teach this yoga when Vivasvat existed a long, long time before?

5) The Blessed Lord said: Many are the births taken by Me and you, O Arjuna. I know them all while you do not, O Parantapa.

Comment: Krishna mentioned to Arjuna earlier that both of them existed before. Now He is adding further to that. He is telling Arjuna that the difference between the two them is that He can remember all the births He has taken while Arjuna cannot! So far, Arjuna sees Krishna only as an ordinary human being – his friend.

6) Though I am unborn, imperishable and the Lord of beings, yet by subjugating My Prakriti, I come into being by My own maya.

Comment: There is a difference between the birth of an ordinary man and an Incarnation of the Lord. The ordinary man is forced by his own natural tendencies to take birth helplessly and suffer the consequences of it. He has no control over it. But the Incarnations of the Lord come to fulfil a special purpose. His birth is a deliberate intervention into the affairs of the world to purge it of its negativity. Whereas They have control over the events of the world, the ordinary man is totally controlled by what happens in the world.

7) Whenever there is decay of Dharma and the rise of adharma, then I embody Myself, O Bharata.

8) For the protection of the good, for the destruction of the wicked and for the establishment of Dharma, I am born age after age.

9) He who knows thus and truly understands My Divine birth and action, having given up the body, does not take birth again, but comes unto Me, O Arjuna.

> *Comment 7-9: There is a Law that governs this planet. It is called Dharma. Earlier, Krishna said that, like everyone else, He also has a duty. Here He is telling us that His duty is to maintain that Law. It is by the proper functioning of that Law that everything is sustained. He now elaborates on what He said that whenever there is a threat to the existence of that Law, He personifies Himself in order to protect it. This He has done many times before, whenever there was a dire global disorder – when the world was in the grip of evil. And He will continue to do so at all times, not only once more.*
>
> *He enlightens Arjuna by explaining to him that whoever understands this mystery of His Divine birth and Divine action, that person, merely by understanding it, crosses the ocean of birth and death!*

10) Freed from passion, fear and anger, filled with Me, taking refuge in Me, purified by penance in the fire of Knowledge, many have entered into My Being.

11) In whatever way men identify with Me, in the same way do I fulfil their desires. O Partha! Men follow My Path in all different ways.

The Yoga of Renunciation of Action in Knowledge

Comment 10-11: He gives hope to mankind that many who have purified themselves and took refuge in Him were liberated. It is a continuous process and is open to all. He responds equally to anyone whatever may be his mode of worship. Here is a reference to the pluralistic spiritual approach which is so necessary to resolve the age-old conflicts based on religious dogmatism.

Here is a declaration which gives the freedom to choose according to one's mental inclination, for in reality every path that is followed is His Path. Those who think that there is only one path are holding on to partial truth as if it is the whole. This ignorance is the cause of disharmony and much suffering.

12) Longing for success of their action on earth, they worship the gods, for quickly is success born of action in this world of man.

Comment: Most people worship the presiding deities of the solar system for material gains which are easily obtained. Because these things are temporary, one always lives with anxiety. One should recognize that there is a higher goal of eternal fulfilment and strive harder to achieve that.

The wise see relativity as a means that is eventually transcended but the ignorant see it as everything that matters in life. To look at the solar deities as having independent existences apart from the Absolute, makes finite whatever they gain through worshiping. But according to the Vedic doctrines, when these deities are accepted as aspects of the Absolute, then there is permanent gain.

13) The fourfold caste was created by Me according to the different varieties of Guna and Karma. Although I am the author thereof, know Me to be the actionless and changeless.

Comment: The four castes are of a social order consisting of different professions. They are Brahmin or teacher, Kshatriya or soldier, Vaisya or industrialist and Sudra or labourer. Krishna is saying that He has created them according to their different tendencies associated with the Gunas. The implication is that each group occupies that particular profession according to their natural aptitude.

The other part relates to the person's conduct in his previous lives (karma). This being so, we may conclude that the principle of inheritance is also involved. His status is due to the merit or demerit of his previous birth. But why cannot one change one's caste-duty for another? The reason was given earlier. The characteristics of each caste have been identified. But what happens if the behaviour of those, belonging to a particular caste, is not consistent with the trait as expected of them? In ancient times there have been examples of persons who have changed from Kshatriya to Brahmin and visa versa but that was exceptional, not general. Generally, the caste-laws were very strict. These duties (social laws) were consistent with the norm of life. Those who did not follow those edicts excluded themselves by their own behaviour from the system that was developed.

It is often argued that the caste-system has divided the society into hundreds of groups and as a result the society has become very weak and inefficient. That may be so, but that does not appear to be the primary objective when it was formed. The basic objective seems more to be the division of labour for the proper functioning of society. It appears that there was a stable society for thousands of years and as a result the country has been highly developed and very prosperous until very recently. There was a community spirit, and sacrifice was promoted as the ideal. Those who refused to follow that ideal excluded themselves from the system. Those who did so were from all the castes. They were the outcaste. In the West there were the outlaws who were pursued and punished. The outcastes were allowed to live their own way of life, but they were looked upon as inferior. Perhaps this is how the 'untouchable' caste

The Yoga of Renunciation of Action in Knowledge

developed. However, Hinduism does not teach that the descendants have to pay for the sins of their forefathers. There is the freedom and encouragement for everyone to improve oneself, and this has been declared very emphatically elsewhere in the Bhagavad Gita.

What is regarded today as the caste system is in reality caste prejudice. This became very strong during the British rule of India. When there was a need to manage the affairs of the British Raj the learned Brahmin and Kshatriya were chosen. With a highly paid salary, quite naturally the envy of others was the inevitable consequence. Thus we have a changing of names to fit in the British parlance – Bandopadhyay became Bannerjee, Chattopadhyay became Chatterjee etc! Previously, there was a sense of Duty. The British introduced a sense of reward! From this sense of reward everyone tries to protect his own interest. Competition that was unknown in the caste society became emphatic as a business strategy! Present day Indians are keen in pursuing that policy. The social consequences are generally not considered.

14) Actions do not taint Me, nor is the fruit of action desired by Me. He who knows Me thus is not bound by actions.

15) Knowing thus, even the ancient seekers after freedom performed action. Therefore you should perform action as did the ancients in the olden times.

Comment 14-15: Krishna is giving a strong emphasis on action as an important form of spiritual activity when performed without expectation of reward. This has got particular relevance for the Hindu society today that gives more importance to anyone who lives in the Himalayan caves than one who is engaged in helping suffering humanity. Again, He draws our attention to the fact that the ancient seekers did follow that path with the implication that we also should follow it. Perhaps even during the time of Krishna there was a tendency to look down upon work as inferior to the pursuit of knowledge and the Path of Devotion. That is why he is drawing our attention to the fact that this Path of Action was followed by the ancients with great success.

16) Sages too are perplexed as to what is action, what inaction. Therefore I shall tell you what action really is and by knowing this you shall be freed from evil.

17) It is necessary for you to discriminate between action, forbidden action, and inaction; mysterious is the way of karma.

> Comment 16-17: The philosophy of action is a unique contribution of the Bhagavad Gita. Nowhere else has action been discussed so thoroughly although it is so central to our existence. Action has been divided in three categories — action, inaction and forbidden action. It is not a simple topic but by fully understanding it, one becomes liberated from the chain of re-action that is connected with these different forms of action. Action is what we do generally being prompted by desire. Forbidden action is what we know is wrong to do, but is done being forced by instinct. Inaction does not mean that we simply do not do anything physically while mentally cogitating on the result. Each of them produces a relative re-action which is linked with the doer.

18) He who sees inaction in action and action in inaction, he is wise among men, he is really a yogi and one who achieves everything.

19) The sages declare that man to be wise whose activities are all free from design and desire for results, and whose actions are all burnt by the fire of knowledge.

20) Having abandoned attachment to the fruits of action, being ever contented and depending on nothing, though he may engage in the performance of karma, verily he does not do anything.

Comment 18-20: The person who can differentiate between what has been mentioned above and the real nature of inaction is a sage whose every action produces results that are beneficial to all since he himself is detached from its fruit as a result of his Self-knowledge. He is therefore free from the sense of doership and the consequences of his action do not cling to him. Hence, though he acts, he is doing nothing i.e. not accumulating merits or demerits.

21) Free from hope, with his mind and self controlled and having given up all his possessions, he who performs karma by using his body alone incurs no sin.

22) Content with what he gets without much effort, free from the pairs of opposites, without envy, balanced in success and failure, though acting, he is not bound.

Comment 21-22: We are told about the things that are the sources of our problems and if we gain control over these sources of attachment we shall experience freedom and peace. One of the basic causes of stress is mental dissatisfaction. With the mind under control and application of the limbs of the body in carrying out one's duties, all tensions from the mind are released.

Contentment is one of the greatest virtues. If there is contentment much of man's unhappiness will disappear. It is the means to get rid of envy, greed and jealousy which are common weaknesses.

23) One who is unattached, liberated, whose mind is absorbed in knowledge and who performs work for Yajna alone, his entire karma melts away.

24) The oblation is Brahman, the clarified butter is Brahman, offered by Brahman into the fire of Brahman; unto Brahman verily he goes who perceives Brahman alone in all his activities.

Comment 23-24: *The substance of Yajna and karma are here explained. Work must be done entirely within the spirit of self-denial in order to transcend negative impact of action which induces man to behave abnormally. Yajna is explained as that in which there is a Divine connection with everything. Perceiving the Divine in all activities liberates one from cause and its effects, because Brahman is the ultimate Source of all. Actually, everyone is acting but without the vision that all beings are connected by an inherent Divinity.*

The conclusion is that one becomes what one meditates on. When the mind is focused on the Divine in all of one's activities, it becomes divinised and this leads to the realization of oneness with the Absolute.

Once a sanyasin and a non-Hindu were discussing.
Non-Hindu: "Do you have a connection with your parents and relations?"

Sanyasin: "No. After a person renounces the world, he no longer has personal connections."

Non-Hindu: "What kind of religion is that? I must have contact with my brother and if my brother's children need help, I must help them."

Sanyasin: "Look at it in this way. Assuming that your brother's children do not have any need and another man's children are in need, will you not help them just because they are not your brother's children? Well. To me every man is my brother and every man's children are like my brother's children."

This is the difference between a person who is attached and one who is non-attached. Attachment narrows our vision. Detachment expands it.

25) Some yogis perform sacrifices to the Devas alone, while others

The Yoga of Renunciation of Action in Knowledge

offer the self as sacrifice by the self verily in the fire of Brahman.

26) Some offer the sense of hearing and other senses as sacrifice in the fire of restraint, while others offer sound and other sense-objects as sacrifice in the fire of the senses.

27) Others again offer all the actions of the senses and the functions of the life-energy, as a sacrifice in the fire of self-control, kindled by knowledge.

28) Yet others offer wealth, austerity and yoga as sacrifice, while still others offer self-denial and extreme vows, some offer sacred study and knowledge as sacrifice.

29) There are others also who sacrifice the outgoing breath in the incoming, and the incoming in the outgoing, restraining the flow of the outgoing and incoming breaths and solely absorbed in the regulation of the life-energy.

30) Still others of regulated food-habit offer in the pranas the functions thereof. All these are knowers of the value of Yajna, because their sins were destroyed by practising Yajna.

> *Comment 25-30: These are all different forms of austerities (tapasya). This ancient ideal of tapasya is presented as Yajna. For in reality both are the same. Tapasya is to go against the inclination of the senses. Fasting, for example, is to practise control over the habit of eating at a particular time so that as soon as that time arrives one feels hungry. By the practice of fasting in the correct way an inner willpower develops. This helps to resist negative habits and ultimately one is purified of all sinful inclinations.*
>
> *The sages knew this and it has been recommended by all the ancient teachings. But modern teachers advocate systems of a comfortable religion. And people are trapped by their likes and dislikes. Rather than becoming detached, they become more attached.*

31) The eaters of the nectar-like remnant of Yajna go to the Eternal Brahman. This world has no place for the non-sacrificer, how can there be any in the other, O best of the Kurus?

Comment: The practice of Yajna is so great that it leads to Brahman who is Absolute. Krishna says that in this world there is no place for the man who does not make sacrifices because no one likes to be next to a scrounger. In the same way there will not be a place for him in the next world after he dies. He will simply be like a rent cloud.

32) Various kinds of Yajnas such as these are to be found in the storehouse of the Vedas. Know them all to be produced from karma; and thus knowing you shall be free.

Comment: The sacred text deals mainly with the principle of Yajna, i.e. how it is beneficial to us in this life and how it releases us from the bondage of the material world. It brings prosperity to us in this life and liberates us as well. All aspirants of ancient times recognised yajna as the basic means to enjoy harmony, peace and freedom.

33) Knowledge-sacrifice, O Scorcher of foes, is superior to wealth-sacrifice. All karma in its entirety, O Partha, culminates in knowledge.

34) Seek that enlightenment by prostrating, by questioning and by service. The wise who are the seers into the Truth will instruct you in that knowledge.

Comment 33-34: The purpose of life is to seek enlightenment. The procedure is to search for the man of realization (the Guru or Master). After meeting him to surrender, then offer service to him. Finally one must ask questions that are relevant to one's spiritual development. Only the seers who are the knower of the Truth can explain it.

The Yoga of Renunciation of Action in Knowledge

Without tapasya (surrender and selfless service) the mind cannot become receptive and therefore whatever the teacher says will either not be retained or is understood in a distorted way.

There is an old story often told to explain how an untutored student can harm himself by book-knowledge or hearsay. He may read or hear something, but does not properly understand the significance of what he has heard or read. As a result he applies what he understands improperly and he harms himself.

The story is about a spiritual Master teaching his students that everything that exists is a manifestation of God in different forms. A lay disciple overheard what the Master had said and was pondering over it as he went along. Just then he heard a Mahout crying: "Beware of this mad elephant!" The Mahout was repeating the same thing as the elephant was moving along and everyone was getting out of the way.

But the lay student thought to himself: "If everything is God, as the teacher has said, then I am God and the elephant also is God. Why should God harm God?" As a result, the elephant caught him and threw him and he hurt his leg. He went back to the teacher and complained that as a result of his false teaching he had a broken leg! When the teacher questioned him, he related what had happened. The teacher said: "My son, my teaching is not at fault. It was because you did not understand properly what I had said that you are now in this pain! You have forgotten that the Mahout also is God. You are suffering because you did not heed the warning of God!"

35) After knowing this, O Pandava, you will not again fall into this confusion. By this you will see the whole of Creation in your self and in Me.

Comment: After proper preparation, that knowledge will be grasped and there will never again be confusion about the nature of things. The greatness of Self-knowledge is that one sees everything in the Lord and in one's own self. When one recognizes all beings in one's own self, how can one harm another? This is the greatness of the mystical teachings of Hinduism and that is the reason why Hindus live in harmony with everyone. To understand one's true relationship with other beings is the only way by which all problems of the world can be solved. There is no other way.

36) Even if you may be the most sinful of all sinners, yet you shall cross over all sins by the raft of knowledge.

37) As the blazing fire reduces fuel to ashes, O Arjuna, so does the fire of knowledge reduce all karma to ashes.
38) Verily, there is no purifier in this world like knowledge. He that is perfected in yoga realises it in his own heart in due course of time.

Comment 36-38: Krishna draws our attention to the greatness of knowledge. However wicked a person may be, knowledge will destroy all his sins in the same way as fire burns a piece of wood to ashes. We do not need greater assurance about the benefit of knowledge. It is the most important thing we can possess. It destroys all problems because it destroys ignorance in the same way as light destroys darkness. When one attains perfection through the practice of Yoga Sadhana, one realises its transforming and peaceful effect.

39) The man of Shraddha, the devoted and he who is master of his senses obtains knowledge. After he gains knowledge he goes promptly to the Peace Supreme.

Comment: There are three things that are necessary in order to attain Self-knowledge. They are steadfast dedication, pure devotion and self-control. As soon as one attains Self-knowledge, one experiences not ordinary peace, but Supreme Peace here in this very life! This is what sacrifices ultimately lead to. Can there be any greater gain?

The Yoga of Renunciation of Action in Knowledge

40) The ignorant, the man devoid of Shraddha, the doubting self, goes to destruction. The doubting self has neither this world, nor the next, nor happiness.

41) With work absolved in yoga, and doubts rent asunder by knowledge, O Dhanajaya, actions do not bind him who is poised in the Self.

42) Therefore, severing with the sword of knowledge this ignorance-born doubt about the Self dwelling in your heart, be established in yoga. Stand up, O Bharata.

> *Comment 40-42: In spite of the great benefits that this Yoga Dharma offers, still there are some who will not make an effort to practise and others who will have their doubts about it. Such people cannot be helped despite the best effort. Eventually they destroy themselves. Blessed are those who are able to overcome this negative weakness. It must be due to merits acquired in previous lives and positive efforts in this life.*
>
> *When the negative effects of work are overcome by the practice of yoga and doubts destroyed by knowledge, one is no longer bound by one's action. Krishna urges Arjuna to make use of knowledge as a weapon and destroy the inner enemy in the form of ignorance which is an obstacle to Self-realization, and also to harmony and peace in this world.*

CHAPTER FIVE

THE YOGA OF RENUNCIATION

1) Arjuna said: O Krishna, you commend the renunciation of action, and at the same time You extol its performance. Please tell me definitely which of the two is better?

> *Comment: Krishna speaks very highly of the Path of Renunciation of action and again the same of the performance action. Earlier, Arjuna told Krishna that he was confused by what He was saying and asked Him to say definitely what was good for him. In the very first verse of this chapter, he again raises a somewhat similar question. He wants to know which is better. He perhaps raised this question with the intention of being able to make a choice. He is not a silent student. He is asking very relevant questions. And the teacher is very pleased with him. This kind of teacher is very difficult to find.*

2) The Blessed Lord said: Both renunciation of action and its performance lead to freedom. But of the two, performance of action is superior to renunciation of action.

> *Comment: Again, Krishna is emphasizing the greatness of action. As far as attaining the final goal of life they are alike. Yet, he regards action as superior. He is raising the discussion to a higher level.*

3) He should be known as a steadfast sanyasin, who neither hates nor desires. O mighty-armed, when he is freed from the pairs of opposites, he effortlessly becomes free from bondage.

4) Only children, not the wise, speak of knowledge and performance of action as different. He who dedicatedly practises one of them gets the fruit of the other as well.

5) The state that is attained by the aspirants after knowledge (Jnanis) is also reached by the yogis who perform action (karma). His understanding is proper who knows that the Path of Knowledge (Jnana Yoga) and the Path of Action (Karma Yoga) are no different.

> Comment 3-5: *He identifies the attitude that helps a renunciate to attain freedom. Only those who are still at a low level, whose vision is still not quite clear, see the Yoga of Knowledge and the Yoga of Action as different. But the wise know that they lead to the same goal.*

6) Sanyasa, O mighty-armed, is hard to attain without the practice of Karma Yoga; the man of meditation, purified by Karma Yoga, quickly goes to Brahman.

7) With the mind purified by Karma Yoga, the self disciplined and the senses subdued, one who realises one's Self as the Self in all beings, though acting, he is not affected.

> Comment 6-7: *The practice of Karma Yoga is an important aid for the aspiring sanyasin, because it is a necessary means to discipline the mind and the senses. As a result of that discipline one experiences the unity of all that exists, and by seeing himself in everything he will not act adversely in order to be affected. To him the whole Creation becomes one family ('vasudaiva kutumbakam'). When the conditioned Self is purified through the practice of self-less activities, the Supreme State is immediately attained.*

8-9) The sage whose mind is centred in the Self should think: "I do nothing at all" – though seeing, hearing, touching, smelling, eating, going, sleeping, breathing, speaking, emptying, holding, opening and closing the eyes – he must be firm in the thought that the senses move among the sense-objects.

> *Comment: In order to maintain constant awareness of his identity with the Atman (Self), the sage must detach himself even from the normal physical activities that go on.*

10) He who acts without attachment and dedicates everything he does to Brahman, is untainted by sin, even as a lotus-leaf is untouched by water.

> *Comment: Krishna again uses a very beautiful simile. When we habitually offer everything we do to the Divine, ultimately our nature becomes so pure because all the negative instincts are cleansed and just as a lotus-leaf is not soiled by dirty water, even so we are not affected by the temptations of the world.*
>
> *We may explain this further. Let's take a cup that is full of poison. If we pour pure water into the cup continuously, all the poison will be eventually emptied with the overflowing of the water and then only pure water will remain. The same thing happens to our nature if we continuously remember the Divine while carrying out our daily duties. By focusing the mind on the Divine, every act becomes a form of worshiping the Divine and, as a result, our whole being becomes sanctified. And when the conditioning factors no longer pollute the nature, we become our true Self, unaffected by the events of the world.*

11) The yogi who abandons attachment performs work with the body, the mind, the intellect and the senses only for self-purification.

> *Comment: With knowledge, the body and the organs can be made use of to one's advantage. This is their purpose. But when one is ignorant, they are being used to one's own disadvantage.*
>
> *When we enter our home in the night, the first thing we do*

The Yoga of Renunciation

is to switch the lights on, otherwise all the lovely furniture that are meant for our comfort, become obstacles on which we hit ourselves in the darkness. Our body is like the home and knowledge is the light that makes our home comfortable. Therefore pursuit after knowledge makes our life happier.

Basically, sadhana is practised for purifying our nature and not for achieving something external. As mentioned elsewhere many are tempted to pray only for material things and not as a form of self-culture.

12) By renouncing the fruit of action, the yogi attains peace that is achieved through steadfastness; induced by desire, the non-yogi is bound by being attached to the fruit.

Comment: The difference between renunciation and attachment and their respective results is clearly defined. Renunciation of the fruit of action leads to peace. The other leads to bondage and the chain of problems that are linked to it. Therefore, it is to our advantage that we follow the Path of Yoga.

13) Having mentally renounced all actions, the self-disciplined Indweller rests happily in the city of nine gates, neither acting nor causing another to act.

Comment: By renouncing doership and the fruit of action, the Atman in the body is happy. When one does not have any expectation nor depends on anyone, no one is forced to do anything for him. Here the city refers to the body with nine openings – the two eyes, the two ears, the two nostrils, the mouth, the reproductive organ and the organ of excretion.

14) The Lord does not create agency or actions for the world; He does not create union with the fruits of action. Nature does all this.

Comment: We are accustomed to think that God directly rewards us for our good or bad deeds. That is not the case. The tendency that these deeds create in our nature acts on its own. Whatever we do mentally or physically is stored in subtle vibrations in our nature causing us to behave accordingly. This makes us as responsible beings and not helpless creatures. If human beings can look at life in this way, they may act less senselessly and the world will really be a better place. To shirk that responsibility, we place the cause of our abnormal behaviour on an external agent and use this as an opportunity to make endless excuses.

15) The Omnipresent does not take note of the merit or demerit of anyone. Knowledge is veiled by ignorance and this is the cause why mortals become deluded.

Comment: How does nature operate in a negative way? That is explained: through ignorance. When we are ignorant, our past action has a full impact upon us. That is why the pursuit of knowledge is important. It helps to mitigate our suffering by taking wise decisions and act wisely.

It is like a person who hears the weather forecast and knows that there is going to be heavy rain and he takes a raincoat and an umbrella with him. Another, who did not hear the forecast, goes unprepared and gets drenched by the rain. He may even catch a cold and suffer for that. Knowledge protects us. It increases our life span and our happiness.

16) Shining like the sun, knowledge reveals the Supreme in them whose ignorance has been destroyed by Self-knowledge.

Comment: Just as the sunrays destroy darkness, similarly Self-knowledge destroys all ignorance. When that happens, the Supreme, Who is always present, becomes revealed. And by such revelation life's purpose has been achieved.

17) Those who think on That, merge in That, get fixed in That,

have That as the Goal, they attain to the state of non-return because the taints of their nature have been purified by knowledge.

> *Comment: The idea of 'Brahma arpanam' mentioned earlier becomes clearer here. In order to develop a continuous consciousness of the Divine pervading everything that exists, one has got to learn to keep the mind in the present because it is by keeping it in the present that it becomes steady. The past and the future have no existence without the present. If we can take care of the present, the past and the future will take care of themselves. By constantly remembering the Divine through repeating the Guru-mantra is one way of keeping the mind stable and remembering the Divine. Gradually, the mind will be free from the images of past and future and be established in the present. As the negative vibrations of past and future that are stored in the subconscious decrease, knowledge of the Self increases. When the nature is completely emptied of desire, which is the basic cause of bondage to birth and death, one does not return to this mortal world again.*

18) Men of Self-knowledge do not discriminate between a Brahmana imbued with learning and humility, a cow, an elephant, a dog and an outcaste.

> *Comment: With Self-knowledge comes the experience of the oneness of existence. No matter what the form is, the basic substance that sustains it is the inherent Divine potential. That in reality is what everything is, but because of ignorance we accept the physical existence as the sole reality. Conditioned by delusion, we do not see our physical bodies as having a relative existence. Hence we differentiate between one thing and another and we label them accordingly. Naam (name) and roop (form) are the basic cause of conditioning. And only Self-knowledge can remove that.*
>
> *Today, we are talking of racial and other forms of*

discrimination. Thousands of years ago the Gita taught that there must not even be discrimination between one being and another. When shall we evolve to that state of consciousness, which is to our greater benefit?

19) Transitory existence is overcome even here by those who focus their minds on equality. Brahman is flawless and the same in all; therefore they are established in Brahman.

Comment: By focusing the mind on unitary existence, one realises the Absolute that is in everything. By that experience one gets liberated from the attachment to this illusory world even while here in this body.

Equal respect for all beings is the way by which we can transform our earth into a heavenly abode.

20) Established in Brahman, with firm understanding and with no delusion, the knower of Brahman rejoices not when he gets what is pleasant, and grieves not when he gets what is unpleasant.

Comment: The pleasant and unpleasant are emotional states based on sense experiences and undergo changes. The Absolute Reality (Brahman) is unchangeable. Therefore, one who realises Brahman is free from the pairs of opposites such as pleasant and unpleasant and consequently is not affected by them.

21) When the self becomes detached from the external contacts, he realises the bliss in the Self. And by constant meditation on Brahman, he enjoys imperishable Bliss.

Comment: Pleasure comes through the enjoyment of material things but blissful experience comes by detachment from material things. And when the senses, mind and intellect (the lower self) become detached from worldly things, a person experiences the bliss of the Self that was always there, but because of attachment to the fleeting objects of the material world the lower self was distracted from the pure bliss of the Self. The impact of this experience makes it possible to remain engrossed in Brahman, the Source of eternal bliss.*

22) The delights that are contact-born are verily the wombs of pain. O son of Kunti, they have a beginning and an end; no wise man takes delight in them.

Comment: Our attention is drawn to the fact that everything which excites us leads to suffering because they are not enduring. And knowing it to be such, one should not indulge in them.

23) He who is able to resist the impulse of desire and anger even here, before he quits the body – he is a yogi; he is a happy man.

24) He whose happiness is within, whose delight is within, whose illumination is within only, that yogi becomes Brahman and gains the Beatitude of Brahman.

Comment 23-24: Material things are not the sources of happiness since they are transitory. Real happiness comes from within. Therefore, resisting the temptations of desire by which anger also is overcome, one becomes happy. That is the yogic state – the attainment of eternal life.

25) When all their sins are destroyed, doubts removed and their minds disciplined, being delighted in the welfare of all beings, the Rishis attain the Beatitude of Brahman.

26) The Beatitude of Brahman is both here and hereafter for those sanyasins who have shed lust and anger, subdued their minds and realised the Self.

Comment 25-26: Earlier Arjuna asked Krishna for signs by which one can know the knower of Brahman. Here we are told that one who is no longer a sinful person, who is a saint, such a person finds happiness in the welfare of all beings. He no longer hates nor is he full of greed and lust. Saintliness is not a matter that is decided after one dies, but it expresses itself here, in this very life.

Krishna here equates the yogi with the Rishi (seer) and the sanyasin (renunciate: one who renounces worldly pleasures). In their quest, they all attain the Supreme Goal because they have been able to subdue their passions which are the result of separation and individual existences.

27) Keep all external objects out from the mind. Fix the gaze between the eyebrows and equalizing the outward and inward breaths moving in the nostrils.

28) That sage is verily liberated who has controlled the senses, mind and intellect, cast away desire, fear and anger and solely pursues the Path to Liberation.

Comment 27-28: Since material objects are the causes by which the mind is disturbed, it is necessary to free the mind from them. But how do we do that? The answer is provided. It is a form of meditation which one should practise regularly. The gaze is to be fixed at the 'root' of the nose and concentrate on the incoming and outgoing breath. The rhythm of the breathing must not be haphazard. For example, if the count is three when breathing in, it must remain the same when breathing out and the in and out going breath must be regular. By this practice the extroverted mind will gradually become introverted. As the mind gradually becomes calmer and more peaceful, desire will slowly disappear and with it, fear and anger. That is the path by which the sages become free from the attachment of worldly entanglement.

29) Knowing Me as the Lord of all Yajnas and asceticism, as the Ruler of all the worlds and the Friend of all beings, he attains peace.

Comment: Krishna finally concludes this chapter on a very fine note. Generally, we think of God as the Greatest and the Mightiest. Here Krishna adds something very significant. God is also the Friend of the whole of Creation. Knowing this, one cannot cause harm to anyone and hope that God will be pleased. In fact, establishing a friendly relationship with all is the way to peace and happiness. If this lesson alone can be taught, our world will be a paradise to live in! In friendship there is no fear. There is trust, something we badly need in our world.

CHAPTER SIX:

THE YOGA OF MEDITATION

1) The Blessed Lord said: He who discharges his duty without seeking its fruit must be known as a sanyasin and a yogi, not he who has given up the sacred Fire and the performance of rites.

> *Comment: Here is an emphasis on duty. There are those who insinuate that a sanyasin is one who simply gives up ritualistic practice and performance of the Fire rites. Krishna is saying that a true yogi or sanyasin is one who performs his duty without expectation of rewards. Sitting in a cave is not the sign of a yogi.*
>
> *There is an old story about a yogi who practised intense austerity. One day he looked at a bird and it was burnt to ashes. After that incident he went to a house begging for alms, but the housewife delayed in opening the door. In anger he looked at her with widely opened eyes. The housewife apologized for the delay by telling him that her husband had just returned from the farm and she was offering him his food when he knocked at the door. She then reprimanded the yogi for his childish behaviour. She said that she could not be burnt the same way as he had burnt the poor bird a while ago. The story goes on to emphasise the greatness of duty. Shirking their responsibilities many escape under the guise of being sanyasins. This is also a caution to the public that just because one claims to have lived in mountain caves, that one has necessarily achieved something special.*
>
> *Acharya Swami Pranavananda of the Bharat Sevashram Sangha*

said that the real mountain cave is a calm and steady mind. When the mind is calm and peaceful, it cannot be attacked by any temptation. One should engage fully in one's duty, irrespective of what that duty is. In duties there is no choice, otherwise it is not duty.

2) Know that as yoga, O Pandava, which is called Sanyasa. None can become a yogi without renouncing of the Sankalpa.

Comment: A sanyasin is one who has renounced all worldly cravings. And unless one detaches one's self from worldly ties, one cannot become a yogi. In this respect there is no difference between renunciation and yoga.

3) The Muni who seeks to attain yoga must follow the Path of Karma. After he has attained to yoga he should pursue the Path of Quietude.

Comment: The renunciate must first fulfil his obligations and then, as he advances towards perfection, he should follow the Path of Silence, i.e. after he no longer has any duties to perform.

4) Yoga is said to be attained only when all the Sankalpas have been renounced and one does not get attached to sense-objects and actions.

Comment: Attachment to material things as well as actions and mental musings has to be overcome before one can attain perfection in yoga. The emphasis is on inner preparation.

5) Let a man raise himself by his own Self; let him not degrade himself. For he himself is his friend or his own enemy.

6) He who has conquered his (base) self by the (divine) Self, his own self is like a friend; but he who has not subdued the self, his own self acts as his foe.

> *Comment 5-6: These two verses make one responsible for one's own destiny. It gives the incentive to make great efforts to elevate oneself. Since his future lies in his own hands, he must work incessantly for a brighter future. These are two of the most encouraging verses. If one meditates on them, they make one like a lion. No time will be spent wastefully. Every moment becomes very important and every act, an act that is creative. He strives to move on and on, without trampling on others which would be negative. Every act, every word and every thought is used in a positive way.*

7) The self disciplined and serene man's Supreme Self is steady in cold and heat, pleasure and pain, and also in honour and dishonour.

8) The steadfast yogi is satisfied with knowledge and wisdom. He remains unshaken and has conquered the senses. To him a lump of earth, a stone and a piece of gold are the same.

9) He stands supreme who has equal regard for friends, companions, enemies, neutrals, arbiters, the hateful, the relatives, saints and sinners.

> *Comment 7-9: When the mind and senses are disciplined, one is not affected by changed circumstances. Since he is not attached to material things nor depends on them, he views everything in the same way.*
>
> *The man who is dependent on material acquirements has a different value system from the man who has renounced everything. He has nothing for anyone to steal or be jealous of, nor does anyone have anything that he would covet.*
>
> *Here is an old story of a couple. They reached the stage of Vanaprastha (retirement in the forest) and they both decided to leave home to live in seclusion in the forest. The husband was walking in front and on the way he saw a lump of gold.*

> *He said to himself: "If my wife sees this, it will be the end of Vanaprastha life"! He went quickly and stood over the gold until his wife came. She then said to him: "How is it that you still make a distinction between a lump of gold and a lump of earth?" The point is that those things only have value to those who are attached to them.*
>
> *Those who are attached make a distinction between close relationships and those who are distant, those who are not related, those who are enemies, etc. As a result of that attachment come love and hate, etc., which are the causes of mental agony. The detached man is the wisest because he is free from such attitude and does not get tormented.*
>
> *The great do not make a distinction between saints and sinners. Yet this is what many preachers of the Semetic religions do in order to Proselytise. By so doing, they create the conditions for division and hatred. To them, everyone, apart from themselves is a sinner*

10) After a yogi has gotten rid of desires and possessions, he should live alone in solitude and always try to concentrate his mind by subduing his senses and body.

> *Comment: Krishna gives a programme of mental preparation for meditation. After that is completed, he must sit down all by himself in an isolated place intent on controlling his body, senses and the mind. He must be solely devoted to his pursuit in Self-realization.*

11) Having firmly fixed his seat in a clean place which is neither too high nor too low, and spread over it kusa-grass, a deer skin and a cloth, one over the other;

12) Sitting there on his seat with one-pointed mind and restraining the thinking-faculty and the senses, he should practise yoga for self-purification.

13) Let him hold the body, head and neck erect and still, gazing at the tip of his nose, without looking about.

> *Comment 11-13: Now, the principles that are involved are presented. First is the preparation of a proper seat on the ground made up of kusa-grass, a deer skin and a piece of cloth. This must be done in a reversed order. The seat must not be too high nor too low. Next is the attitude: it is not for gaining anything, but it is practised for self-purification — just like we take a bath to clean and refresh our body. With such care, the body will remain healthy. We do not think about the health-aspect until we become ill. We just feel refreshed after a bath. It is a natural thing. Similarly, meditation must be practised with a detached attitude — not for acquiring anything, but to get rid of something which creates an obstacle to Self-realization.*
>
> *Next, the body posture must be upright and still for a period of time. The period should be increased gradually. The gaze must be fixed at the tip of the nose without looking in any other direction so that concentration will not be disturbed. It is necessary to maintain this posture as long as possible without being too uncomfortable. Those who cannot sit on the ground may sit on a low stool. A too soft or spongy seat can prevent one from sitting erect.*

14) Serene, fearless and firm in the vow of a Brahmachari, and being subdued in mind, he should sit in yoga thinking of Me and be intent on Me alone.

> *Comment: Fear is the cause of fickle-mindedness and lack of concentration. The mind must be calm and quiet and focused on the Lord. A celibate life forms the foundation for self-culture and a steady mind, and it is particularly emphasized here for one who aspires to attain perfection in yoga.*

15) Being ever steadfast in this manner, the yogi of subdued mind attains peace, abiding in Me and culminating in Nirvana.

The Yoga of Meditation

Comment: By devotedly following this procedure set out above, the fickleness of the mind is overcome. Then that peace, which is the essential nature of the Lord, is attained. When that happens, there is complete freedom. The Lord is the Embodiment of Peace, and by worshiping Him, a peaceful nature is the surest sign that our devotion is properly placed. Otherwise, it is all mechanical, a mere showmanship. We are assured elsewhere that in this practice of Yoga Dharma, there is no loss of effort or any contrary result.

16) Yoga is not possible for him who eats too much or abstains too much from eating; it is not for him, O Arjuna, who sleeps too much or too little.

17) But for him who is moderate in eating, recreation and action, who is regulated in sleep and wakefulness, yoga becomes the destroyer of pain.

Comment 16-17: Moderation is emphasized as the basic approach in the lifestyle of those who practise yoga. If that is pursued, yoga becomes a healer of all diseases. Such regulated practice helps one to become conscious of what one is doing, otherwise there might be a tendency to do things mechanically and habitually. One must develop the spirit of Self-consciousness.

Suffering is a negative experience to be overcome and not to be idolized. To prevent suffering is one of the greatest drives in history. Yoga is not only preventative but curative as well. It is good for our body, mind and spirit.

18) When the disciplined mind rests in the Self alone, free from desire for sense-objects, then one is said to be established in yoga.

19) 'As a lamp in a windless place does not flicker' – this is the simile used for the disciplined mind of a yogi practising concentration on the Self.

20) When the mind attains quietude through the discipline of yoga practice, and when beholding the Self by the self, he is satisfied in the Self;

21) When he experiences that supreme bliss which is perceived by the intelligence and which transcends the senses, wherein established he never moves from the Reality;

22) And gaining which he thinks there is no greater gain than that, established in which he is not shaken even by the heaviest affliction;

23) Let this disconnection from the union with pain be known as yoga. This yoga should be practised with firm determination and with an undistracted mind.

> *Comment 18-23: When the mind is empty of desire for material objects and finds happiness only in contact with the Self, then it is firmly established in yoga. Otherwise it can be practised merely as a convenient means to achieve certain physical benefits.*
>
> *An example is given to us to explain the state of the mind that is reached by one who practises yoga steadfastly. Apart from the physical benefits, the mind itself becomes steady which is the end of all problems! We may have all material possessions, but the mind can still be in a disturbed state. Our happiness depends on our state of mind.*
>
> *By yoga practice the body, senses and mind become constrained and ultimately attuned to ananda (the blissful state) of the Absolute Reality. One of the definitions of the Absolute is that It is changeless. Therefore, after attaining such a state, suffering has no impact upon us. What other achievement can be greater than that? Yoga must be known as that which liberates us from all suffering! Since our pursuit in life is to overcome suffering and yoga offers that advantage,*

wisdom tells us that we should make it the most essential thing of our life.

24) Abandon without reserve all desires born of Sankalpa and curb all the senses from every side by the mind.

Comment: Let no cogitating thoughts which produce desire enter the mind, and keep the senses under control so that stability can be maintained. The repetition of Mantra-japa is one of the most effective ways in doing this as mentioned by the sages.

25) With his intellect set firmly, let him attain quietude little by little. Let him fix the mind on the Self and think of nothing else.

Comment: When one's understanding is not disturbed by any means, the mind remains stable. One must then sit still and meditate on the inner Self regularly.

26) Whatever may cause the wavering and unsteady mind to wander away, let him restrain it from that and subjugate it solely to the Self.

Comment: Whenever sense-objects attract the mind, restrain it by contemplating on the inner Self. It is first necessary to be aware of the sitting posture. As this awareness develops, we become more Self-conscious as the mind detaches itself from the external world. By constant practice it becomes natural and one will soon be able to experience peace. Contemplation on the Self then becomes more natural.

27) Supreme Bliss verily comes to that yogi whose mind is calm, free from passions, sinless and who has become one with Brahman.

28) By constantly engaging the mind in this way, the yogi who is free from sin attains with ease the infinite bliss of contact with Brahman.

29) With his mind harmonized by yoga, he sees himself in all beings and all beings in himself; he sees the same Divine in all.

30) He who sees Me everywhere and sees all in Me, he never loses hold of Me, nor do I become lost to him.

31) He who is established in oneness, worships Me abiding in all beings. That yogi lives in Me, whatever may be his mode of living.

> *Comment 27-31: In these verses, Krishna tells Arjuna what the wonderful result is by practising yoga. In the beginning we are told not to seek results of fleeting objects which cause mental instability and pain. Self-indulgence is the cause of suffering. Self-restraint leads to eternal bliss.*
>
> *This experience is not only personal. It has got a universal impact, because he who sees himself existing in all beings cannot harm anyone without harming himself. Only by the application of such education can we have world peace.*
>
> *The great lesson is to worship God as dwelling in all beings, not somewhere else in the sky. Therefore, we cannot hurt any being without hurting God. It is wrong to think that the slaughtering of others can please God.*
>
> *The teachings in these few verses are very inspiring and one would greatly benefit by sitting calmly and meditating on them.*

32) That yogi, O Arjuna, is regarded as the supreme, who judges pleasure or pain everywhere by the same standard he applies to himself.

> *Comment: The golden rule is to judge the pain we cause to others by applying it to our own self. According to the Mahabharata: 'What we do not like for ourselves, we should not do to others. That, in essence, is what Dharma teaches. Anyone who acts differently does so by yielding considerations other than*

Dharma'. This great teaching is repeated again here in the Gita. It is the essence of all teachings.

33) Arjuna said: O Madhusudhana! I do not see any stability for this yoga of equanimity taught by You because of restlessness.

34) O Krishna! The mind by nature is restless, turbulent, strong and obstinate. I deem it as hard to control as the wind.

> *Comment 33-34: Arjuna speaks here for the ordinary man. We all say the same thing and excuse ourselves from trying! We are living in a selfish world full of short-sightedness. Everyone looks for immediate advantage at the cost of others. We pass laws against discrimination! We know that it is the right way forward, but we will not sacrifice our self-centredness even though we recognize that it is the basic cause of all the problems.*
>
> *There is no possibility to control the obstinate mind. There is no place for this teaching of Yours! This is Arjuna's conclusion.*

35) The Blessed Lord said: I agree, O mighty-armed that the mind is restless and hard to control; but by practice and non-attachment, O son of Kunti, it can be controlled.

36) Yoga is hard to attain, I concede, by a man who cannot control himself; but he who has controlled himself and who strives by right means can attain it.

> *Comment: 35-36: Krishna did not say: No, you are wrong, Arjuna! The great Teacher conceded but explains that there is still a way! It can be attained by correct practice and through non-attachment. The proof lies in practice. That is science. If you carry out the experiment correctly, you will get the right result. In the beginning the result of what is explained might seem doubtful. Like material science, yoga also has laid down the rules to be followed. Krishna assured us earlier that there are no contrary results!*

37) Arjuna said: If a man is possessed of faith but he is unable to control himself and his mind deviates from yoga; having failed to attain perfection in yoga what end does he meet, O Krishna?

38) Being deluded in the Path of Brahman and fallen from both, does he not perish like a rent cloud, without any support, O mighty-armed?

39) Please dispel this doubt of mine completely, O Krishna, for there is none but You who can do this.

Comment 37-39: Arjuna's question has a bearing on the materialistic and spiritual aspects of life – the life of self-indulgence and the life of self-restraint. One has tried to give up all pleasures by following the Path of Restraint. But in the pursuit, if one dies before attaining the goal, is that not a great loss? One did not enjoy the pleasures of the world nor the bliss of immortal life. Then, what is the use of making the effort?

40) The Blessed Lord said: O Partha, neither in this world nor in the next is there destruction for him, for, the doer of good, O My son, never comes to grief.

41) Having attained to the worlds of the righteous and lived there for countless years, he who falls from yoga is reborn in the house of the pure and prosperous.

42) Or he may even be born in a family of wise yogis, but such a birth is verily difficult to obtain in this world.

43) There he regains the knowledge acquired in his former body, and he strives more than he did before for perfection, O joy of the Kurus.

44) By that very former practice he is led on in spite of himself. Even he who merely wishes to know of yoga is superior to the performer of Vedic rites.

45) The yogi who strives with assiduity, purified from sins and perfected through many births, reaches then the Supreme Goal.

> *Comment 40-45: Arjuna's question is relevant to those who believe that this is the only life we have and death is the end of all aspirations. But Krishna assured Arjuna that those who do good will never perish. There is a continuity of life in which all past fruits of action are carried over to the next life and in which case the person is born in a righteous family, which facilitates him to pursue the goal with greater steadfastness than before. Birth in the family of yogis is very rare indeed. Prompted by the inner urge from previous births, the aspirant works harder and ultimately attains Brahman, the Absolute Reality which is the end of rebirths.*
>
> *The Lord gives so much importance to yoga that He declares that the mere intention of one to practise it makes him greater than one who performs rituals all his life. The implication is that the rituals are performed mechanically as if the mere performance of it guarantees the result. Self-improvement is least considered. Whereas, yoga aims at purifying the nature of man, which ultimately leads to self-perfection or enlightenment.*

46) The yogi is deemed superior to ascetics and even to men of knowledge; he is also superior to ritualists. Therefore be you a yogi, O Arjuna.

47) I consider that yogi to be the most devout of all yogis who worships Me with faith and whose inmost Self is merged in Me.

> *Comment 46-47: Arjuna is urged to become a yogi, because a yogi makes independent and steadfast effort. He does not wait or depend on anyone. Of all the yogis, the one who worships the Lord with his whole heart, thinking of none else, is considered the greatest because the Lord is his sole refuge.*

CHAPTER SEVEN:

THE YOGA OF KNOWLEDGE AND REALISATION

1) The Blessed Lord said: Listen, O Partha, how – with your mind clinging to Me, taking refuge in Me and practising yoga – you will without doubt know Me in full.

2) I shall teach you in full this knowledge combined with realization and when known, nothing more here remains to be known.

> *Comment: What a wonderful Teacher! Some Gurus make sure the disciples do not know too much otherwise their own position will become untenable. But Krishna says that He is going to give Arjuna complete knowledge and after knowing that nothing more is to be known! This ideal Teacher is very difficult to find. Of course, only Krishna can impart that supernal knowledge. The greatness of that knowledge is that it is combined with experience. It is not only knowing but being and becoming as well.*

3) Among thousands of men scarcely one strives for perfection, and among those who strive and succeed, hardly one of them knows Me in truth.

> *Comment: Most people worship the Supreme Being for some material benefit. But there are some who do strive sincerely for perfection. Those are the ones who follow the Path of Yoga for self-purification, not to gain some powers. Even among them merely one may know GOD in fullness. Even great*

The Yoga of Knowledge and Realisation

saints may have only a partial view of that Supreme Being. But even that partial experience gives them great happiness.

4) Earth, water, fire, air, ether, mind, intellect and egoism; this is the eightfold division of My Prakriti.

5) This is My lower Prakriti, but different from it, O mighty-armed, is My higher Prakriti – the life element by which this Universe is upheld.

6) Know that these two are the womb of all beings. I am the origin and dissolution of the whole Universe.

7) There is nothing whatsoever higher than Me, O Dhananjaya. All this is joined on Me, like rows of gems on a string.

> *Comment 4-7: The manifested world as we see it is the lower self of the Lord, but that is sustained by the Lord's higher Self. In case we get the impression that there are two selves, the Lord explains that He is the ultimate Source. To the five primal elements that we know, the ego is added. And these make up the material aspect of that Being known as Prakriti. But there is another aspect, which is the life force, which sustains everything that exists. These two are the sources from which everything comes into existence and is being sustained. That Being is the Source of these two and in the end they return back to their original source. In reality, everything that we know has a relative existence and must one day cease to exist as we know it.*
>
> *That Being is infinite. Beyond It nothing exists. In truth, there is no 'beyond' because there is no space!*

8) I am the sapidity in water, O son of Kunti, the radiance in moon and sun; I am the syllable Om in all the Vedas; sound in ether and manliness in man.

9) I am the sweet fragrance in earth and the brilliance in fire; I

am the life in all beings and the austerity in ascetics.

10) Know Me, O Partha, as the eternal seed of all beings; I am the intelligence of the intelligent; the splendour of the splendid.

11) I am the strength of the strong devoid of desire and passion. In beings I am desire, which is not contrary to Dharma, O chief of the Bharatas.

> *Comment 8-11: In these verses Krishna is talking about the essential nature of everything as Divine. This understanding is necessary to recognize how a unitary Divine Power is sustaining diversity, and focusing on that Power can help us to be aware of how everything is inter-connected. This will then have a positive impact on our consciousness, which will help us to live in harmony and peace. Our attitude to nature and other forms of life will be more reverential. Unless we develop that attitude we cannot experience real peace.*

12) And whatever beings there are of Sattva, of Rajas or of Tamas, know them to proceed from Me; still I am not in them, although they are in Me.

> *Comment: Krishna identifies Himself with that Power which is the Source of all that exists. The three Gunas are the manifested aspect of the inner Divine Power. The 'trinity' (three Gunas of Prakriti) manifest in manifold ways, creating a diverse Universe. This Universe does not exhaust that Divine Power. It is merely a speck of It. Therefore, Krishna says that although they are in Me, I am not in them.*

13) Deluded by these threefold dispositions (Gunas) of Prakriti this world does not know Me, Who is above them and immutable.

14) Verily, this Divine illusion of Mine, made up of the Gunas, is hard to overcome; but those who take refuge in Me alone, they cross over this state of illusion.

15) The evil-doers, the deluded, the lowest of men, deprived of discrimination by Maya and following the way of the Asuras, do not seek refuge in Me.

> *Comment 13-15: Diversity creates an illusion because man is attracted by names and forms and forgets the real substance. The objective of prayer, worship and meditation is to focus the mind on that Divine Power – and to that extent that one succeeds, one has also overcome the delusion. Those who are deeply affected by the illusion think that nothing else exists and seek satisfaction in materialism. They are known as Asuras. Maya means a conditioned state through which we are deceived into thinking that the fleeting phenomenal world is real.*

16) Four types of virtuous men worship Me, O Arjuna: the man in distress, the man seeking knowledge, the man seeking wealth and the man imbued with wisdom.

17) Of these, the wise man excels, being ever steadfast and devoted. I am supremely dear to the wise and he is dear to Me.

18) All of these are indeed noble, but the wise man I deem to be My very Self. For he of steadfast mind is established in Me alone, as the Supreme Goal.

19) At the end of many births, the man of wisdom takes refuge in Me, realizing that Vasudeva is all That Is. Rare indeed is that great Soul.

> *Comment 16-19: There are four kinds of devotees. Three of them worship for some favours. Those who are in distress, i.e. particularly those suffering from a disease or in want of a child, they pray to achieve their objectives. Those who are unintelligent pray for knowledge. Those who are in poverty pray for wealth. These people can easily be exploited by charlatans because, rather than focusing on the Divine and*

> surrendering to His Will, they look for quick success and, as a result, can be cheated.
>
> Among them is the man of wisdom. He knows that there are natural causes for suffering and to find a permanent cure for all the problems, one has got to turn to the Source that is the permanent solution. To him those things have only relative importance. He does not worship for any possession. To realise the Divine is all that matters to him – after achieving which nothing more remains to be achieved! Others still remain bound to the womb of pain.

20) But those go to other gods whose discrimination has been led astray by this or that desire and by following this or that rite, constrained by their own nature.

21) Whatever form any devotee with faith wishes to worship, I make that faith of him steady.

22) Endowed with that faith, he engages in the worship of that form, and from it he obtains his desires, which actually are being ordained by Me.

23) But the fruit that accrues to those men of small intellect is finite. The worshippers of the gods go to the gods; My devotees come to Me.

> **Comment 20-23:** These three verses refer to the choices a devotee makes in selecting a deity for worshiping with the intention of satisfying his desire. These choices are made according to one's natural disposition. They are not guided by wisdom. But in reality it is the Lord who stabilizes the faith of that devotee in the deity he worships and because of that he is being rewarded.
>
> Because of ignorance the devotee thinks that the deity he worships has a separate existence from the Absolute and

The Yoga of Knowledge and Realisation

worships only for things of temporary value. As a result, the goal also becomes temporary because whatever one focuses the mind on one attains.

24) Men of poor understanding think of Me, the Unmanifest, as having manifestation, not knowing My Supreme State which is immutable and unsurpassed.

25) I am not revealed to all, as I am veiled by Yoga Maya. This deluded world knows Me not who is Unborn, the Unchangeable.

26) I know, O Arjuna, all beings of past, present and future, but no one knows Me.

27) Deluded by the pairs of opposites arising from desire and aversion, all beings, O Bharata, are subject to illusion at the time of birth.

> *Comment 24-27: We see Krishna as the Son of Devaki. This earthly form is relative. But we cannot think of Krishna without this form. However, in reality, He transcends all forms. He is unborn, the Knower of all who have been, are now, and will be. But with our finite mind, we cannot comprehend the Infinite! Moreover, the mind is always in a state of conflict because we are attached to likes and dislikes from the time we are born. These are natural tools to protect us as we grow. But unless we outgrow them at some stage, we shall never be liberated.*

28) But those men of virtuous conduct, whose sins have come to an end and who are freed from the delusion of the pairs of opposites, worship Me and remain steadfast in their vows.

29) Those who take refuge in Me and strive to overcome decay and death, they realise in full that Brahman, the individual self and all karma.

Comment 28-29: *These verses summarise the results of what happens when one pursues the Path of Yoga Sadhana. All the difficulties one might have encountered on the way become justified. All the delusions and the problems of decay and death are overcome as we progress in achieving our final Goal.*

30) Those who realise Me in the Adhibhuta, in the Adhidhaiva and in the Adhiyajna, they of steadfast mind realise Me even in the hour of death.

Comment: Final verse of this chapter opens up the discussion for the next chapter and therefore does not need to be discussed here.

CHAPTER EIGHT:

THE YOGA OF THE IMPERISHABLE BRAHMAN

1) Arjuna said: What is that Brahman? What is Adhyatma? What is karma? O best among men! What is said to be Adhibhuta, and what is called Adhidaiva?

2) Who and how is Adhiyajna here in this body, O Madhusudana? And how, at the time of death, art Thou to be known by the self-controlled?

> *Comment 1-2: This chapter opens with several queries by Arjuna relating to very important and abstruse topics. The last one is of particular interest, because it is centred on a subject that is of greatest concern to mortal human beings.*

3) The Blessed Lord said: The Imperishable is Brahman, the Supreme. When It dwells in the individual body it is called Adhyatma. The offering which causes the birth of beings is called karma.

4) Adhibhuta relates to the perishable Nature and Purusha is the Adhidaivata. Know Me alone to be the Adhiyajna here in this body, O best of the embodied.

> *Comment 3-4: Krishna gives a precise explanation of the topics. Desire is the cause of birth. Even acts of worshiping, when they are done with desire, create attachments which lead to rebirth. They are called karma. But nishkama karma (desireless action) frees one from rebirths.*

Adhidaivata is nature that is perishable, and Adhidaiva is Purusha Who is Imperishable and the Controller of nature. Adhiyajna in all bodies means the Atman that sustains the body. Though It is sustaining the body, It is known as the Silent Witness of all activities. It does not participate, but remains detached while nature (Prakriti) performs all actions. That inactive involvement is Yajna.

5) And whoever at the time of death, when leaving this body, goes forth remembering Me alone, he comes to Me; there is no doubt about this.

6) Whatever being a man thinks of at the last moment when he leaves his body, that alone does he attain, O Kaunteya, being ever absorbed in the thought thereof.

7) Therefore, at all times think of Me only and fight. With your mind and intellect fixed on Me, you will surely come to Me.

Comment 5-7: Here is a piece of logic. Lord Krishna says that there should be no doubt that whosoever remembers Him when dying will go to Him. Because there is an eternal principle that whatever one thinks about at the last moment, that will decide his future birth!

This is a very important statement: the last thought decides the future birth. Since the mind is conditioned by the way we conduct ourselves, the last thought will depend on the way we live our life. All our past deeds catch up with us in the end. Therefore, at every moment we must think of the Divine while carrying out our duties. By so doing the nature will become divinized and the mind will remain focused on the Divine at the time of death. This is an infallible principle.

Sometimes we think that we have so many things to do, that we do not have time to think of the Divine. But here we find Arjuna on the battlefield, surrounded by enemies on whom he

The Yoga of the Imperishable Brahman

> had to concentrate in order to protect himself. Yet, Krishna advises him not to forget him while fighting! This is an important lesson for us as well. We all have to face that last moment. Therefore, it is to our own benefit that we make proper use of every moment of the time while we are still alive. Even before death we have to face a period of time in a physically helpless state, but the mind is still active. During that period our past haunts us unless our mind is focused on the Divine.

8) He reaches Him, O Partha, whose mind becomes steadfast by constant practice of yoga and not wandering after anything else, and who meditates on the Supreme, resplendent Purusha.

9-10) The Omniscient, the Ancient, the Ruler, minuter than an atom, the Supporter of all, of form inconceivable, effulgent like the sun, and beyond all darkness; he who meditates on this Resplendent, Supreme Purusha, at the time of death, with a steady mind, devotion and strength of yoga, well fixing the entire Prana in the middle of the eyebrows, he reaches Him.

> *Comment 8-10:* Yoga practice includes self-restraint and meditation as its basis. By practising these, the mind becomes steady. Constant meditation on the unchangeable Supreme Purusha ultimately clears the way that is blocked by mental images and the aspirant experiences oneness with Him.
>
> This is a remarkable description of the Purusha, revealing His omniscience, all-pervasiveness, effulgence and the support of everything. The method to be followed in order to realise Him at the time of death has been stated.

11) I shall briefly declare That to you, which the knowers of Veda call the Imperishable, and into which enter the sanyasins who are self-controlled and freed from attachment and desire, leading a life of continence.

12-13) With all the gates of the body closed, and the mind fixed within the heart and the life-energy in the head, firm in the practice of yoga, uttering the monosyllable 'Om' – Brahman – and thinking of Me, he who departs from the body, attains the Supreme Goal.

> *Comment 11-13: Krishna now declares the objective which induces the sanyasins (renunciates) to practise self-control, non-attachment and celibacy, i.e. renouncing all worldly pleasures. By such practices and uttering the mantra 'OM' and concentrating on Him, they reach the Supreme Goal, never to return to this mortal world again. They have fulfilled the purpose of their human birth.*

14) I am easily attainable, O Partha, by that ever steadfast yogi, who constantly remembers Me daily and thinks of none else.

15) Having come to Me, the great Souls are no more subject to rebirth which is transitory and the abode of pain, for they have reached the highest perfection.

> *Comment 14-15: The secret is to remember the Divine all the time. This is the means to get rid of the problems of life and to purify one's nature, thereby becoming one's pure Self. Those moments when we remember the Divine are real moments of life, the truly creative moments of our life. Forgetting the Divine is real death.*

16) All worlds, including that of Brahma, are subject to return but on reaching Me, O son of Kunti, there is no rebirth.

17) Those who know that the day of Brahma lasts a thousand Yugas and that His night lasts a thousand Yugas, they are the real knowers of day and night.

18) At the coming of day all beings proceed from the Unmanifested, and at the coming of night they again merge in the Unmanifested.

The Yoga of the Imperishable Brahman

19) In spite of themselves, this multitude of beings come forth again and again. They merge at the approach of night, and re-manifest themselves at the approach of day.

> *Comment 16-19: The world of Brahma refers to the unmanifest state of existence. From that unmanifest state emerges our Cosmos. There is a constant movement of beings from this manifested world to that which is unmanifest. It goes on for one full Brahma year. In the same way as our year consists of 365 days, Brahma's year is also divided. His year consists of a thousand Yugas and His night consists of another thousand. Therefore, His day, in our sense, consists of 2,000 Yugas. At the end of Brahma's day the whole Cosmos dissolves and a process of recreation starts again after some time. This process has been going on endlessly. In reality there is no end to the world. It is re-cycling itself continuously.*

20) But beyond the unmanifest, there is yet another Unmanifest Eternal Existence which does not perish even when all other existences perish.

21) This Unmanifested is called the Imperisable; It is said to be the Ultimate Goal. Those who attain It return not to the transitory worlds. That is My Supreme Abode.

22) That Supreme Purusha, O Partha, is attainable by unswerving devotion to Him alone, within Whom all beings dwell and by Whom all this is pervaded.

> *Comment 20-22: While there is a constant movement between the Unmanifest and the Manifest, there is another state of existence which is not affected by the changes and that is the Supreme State. This Supreme State is referred to as Unmanifest Eternal Existence which, unlike all other states of existences, does not perish. It is said to be the Ultimate Goal of life and the Supreme Abode of the Divine. That Supreme Divine (Purusha) is all-pervasive and is within all beings.*

Devotion to this immanent aspect of the Divine leads to the Goal of no return. It is worthwhile noting that the Abode of the Lord is not exclusive otherwise that would also be finite, temporary.

This is remarkable! There is an implication that devotion to the Lord as an individual may lead to return back to this world and that the highest form of worship is through devotion to the Lord dwelling in all beings. If this is adopted, there cannot be any problem in the world. The basic conflict in the world is based on a perception of a God who exists above the world and the Creation is like His slave, who must follow His dictates in spite of the suffering it causes to others. According to Krishna, these men of poor intellect are causing the God, who dwells in the body of beings, to suffer by their acts of violence. This violence in the name of God has been going on for centuries. Millions and millions of people have suffered and unless there is an understanding that the Divine dwells within everyone and everything, the world will always remain in a state of conflict. Truces will always be temporary halts in the process.

23) Now I shall tell you, O the best of the Bharatas, about the time in which the yogis depart never to return again, and also about the time in which they depart but return again.

24) Fire, light, daytime, the bright half of the moon, and the six months of the northern path of the sun, going forth then, the knowers of Brahman go to Brahman.

25) Smoke, night, the dark half of the moon, and the six months of the southern passage of the sun, then going forth, the yogi obtains the lunar light and returns.

26) The bright and the dark paths are deemed to be the world's eternal paths. A man goes by one, never to return, but by the other he returns again.

The Yoga of the Imperishable Brahman

27) Knowing these paths, O Partha, no yogi becomes deluded. Therefore, O Arjuna, be steadfast in yoga at all times.

28) The yogi who knows this, transcends the fruits of meritorious deeds attached to the study of the Vedas, sacrifices, austerities and gifts, and attains to the Supreme primeval Abode.

> *Comment 23-28: Krishna explains to Arjuna the two timeless paths that a man follows after he dies. The Path of Desirelessness leads to no return, but when there is still worldly desire in the heart when one dies, he returns again. The Bright Path is that of the pure, and the dark of the impure. The followers of the Path of Yoga are aware of them and never become confused.*
>
> *The practice of religion brings merit. It gives us a sense of direction of how to live in the world based on certain rules. These guidelines are important while a man is undeveloped. But when he is developed he does not need them. It is just like a man driving a car to a particular destination: if he does not know the route, he uses a map until he gets there and then he puts the map away. The yogi is free from evil and he also transcends the good. Therefore, he is fit for that Supreme primal Abode.*
>
> *In the Mahabharata we are told a story about Bhishma while he was a youth. Because of the sacrifice he made for his father's happiness, he was granted a boon that he could not die until he willed it. During the war he was hit by many arrows and when he fell, the arrows formed a bed that sustained him above the ground. There he lay for several days until it was the bright half of the moon when he decided to give up the body.*

CHAPTER NINE:

THE YOGA OF THE HIGHEST SCIENCE AND SUPREME SECRET

1) The Blessed Lord said: To you who do not ask trivial questions, I shall surely declare this, the most profound knowledge combined with realization and by knowing which you will be released from evil.

> *Comment: Krishna sees that Arjuna is a good disciple who is willing to learn. This is a great encouragement to a teacher. He therefore decides to impart the knowledge unreservedly. He declares that he is going to teach him that intuitive knowledge which leads to realization and will liberate him from all evil tendencies. This first verse of the chapter is very inspiring. Arjuna waits expectantly.*

2) This is the sovereign science, the sovereign secret and the supreme purifier. It is directly realizable, consistent with Dharma, very easy to practise and imperishable.

> *Comment: This knowledge is not based on a system of beliefs. It is most scientific and is established on exalted principles. It cannot be easily discovered and there is nothing more purifying – it cleanses the impurity not only of this birth but millions of previous births as well! To acquire it does not depend on a mediator. Although it is abstruse, it is open to anyone who approaches it directly or through a qualified teacher or Guru. Moreover, it is not something new but already based on the sacred Law (Dharma). Although it is very profound, it is very*

The Yoga of the Highest Science

simple to practise! This knowledge is there all the time, but it is hidden by the primal illusion.

3) Men devoid of Shraddha for this Dharma do not attain Me, O oppressor of the foes, but return to the path of the mortal world.

> *Comment: Men who disregard this sacred Law of co-existence (Dharma) do not attain to that Supreme Abode of no return to this mortal world. Adharmic people make life in this world into a hell and if they go to a blissful world after death, they will make that also into another hell! By their attitude and action they exclude themselves from the Supreme Abode. But those, who make this world into a paradise by following the Path of Dharma, directly inherit a place in the Supreme Abode.*

4) This entire Universe is pervaded by Me in My unmanifested form. All beings exist in Me, but I do not abide in them.

5) Nor do the beings dwell in Me. Behold the mystery of My Divine Yoga! Although I bring forth and support these beings, I do not dwell in them.

6) As the mighty wind, that moves everywhere, rests in the Akasa, know that all beings rest in Me.

> *Comment 4-6: The whole Universe is pervaded by the Divine in His unmanifest form, and although He is the cause and support of beings that take birth in this world, the mystery is that they exist in Him but He is not in them, because Creation is only a mere atom of what He is.*
>
> *The mystery is explained by an analogy of the ether that is all-pervasive, enveloping all things yet remaining untouched by them. Similarly, the Divine remains detached although involving in the process of creating.*

7) O Kaunteya, all beings go into My Prakriti at the end of a Kalpa. I generate them again at the beginning of the next Kalpa.*

8) By animating My Prakriti, I send forth all this multitude of beings again and again, being helpless under the power of Prakriti.

9) Nor do these acts bind Me Who remains like One indifferent and unattached to these acts.

10) Because of My Presence, Prakriti produces all things that are moving and unmoving. As a result of this the world is revolving, O son of Kunti.

> *Comment 7-10: Krishna is saying that at the end of every Kalpa all beings (the whole Universe) return back to their Source which is the Divine womb (Prakriti) of the Lord, and at the beginning of the Kalpa they are again produced into the world. In this way nature acts as an instrument of the Lord in the process of regeneration. This happens by the mere Presence of the Lord and there is no direct contact. It happens spontaneously in an unending process. For further explanation see appendix.*

11) The foolish think of Me as one with a human form, not knowing My higher nature as the Great Lord of all beings.

12) Of vain hopes, actions and knowledge and being devoid of discrimination, they verily partake of the delusive nature of Rakshasas and Asuras.

> *Comment 11-12: Seeing the Lord in human guise, some think of Him as an ordinary man and therefore take no notice of what He teaches. They are not aware of His transcendental nature that is beyond all forms. They develop a materialistic attitude and engage in the pursuit of pleasure. The life of such persons is devoid of merit. Everyone's attitude to life depends*

on what his nature is. As his nature is, so is his attitude. The objective of spiritual pursuit is to purify the nature. In accordance to the degree of change in one's nature, one's behaviour also becomes more enlightened.

13) But the Mahatma, O Partha, partaking of the Divine nature, worship Me with a single mind, knowing Me as the immutable and the Source of all beings.

14) Glorifying Me always, they strive firm in vows, prostrate before Me and worship Me with steadfast devotion.

Comment 13-14: But the great souls of Divine nature, realizing the Lord as the Source of all beings, take refuge in Him and worship Him with a concentrated mind, steadfast devotion and firm vows. Just as the lotus-flower growing in a muddy pool reaches upwards and is not affected by the condition of the pool, similarly these holy men live in the world but are not affected by its negativity.

15) There are others who perform the Sacrifice of Knowledge and worship Me in various ways as the One, as the Distinct and as the All-faced.

16) I am Kratu, I am Yajna, I am Svadha, I am the medicinal herb, I am Mantra, I am also the clarified butter, I am fire, I am oblation.

17) I am the Father of this world, the Mother, the Dispenser and the Grandfather. I am the knowable, the Purifier, the syllable Om and also the Rik, the Saman and the Yajus (Vedas).

18) I am the Goal, the Supporter, the Lord, the Witness, the Abode, the Shelter, the Friend, the Origin, the Dissolution, the Foundation, the Treasure-house and the Seed Imperishable.

Comment 15-18: Everyone worships the Lord according to his natural tendency. Some look at Him in a very personal way and worship Him as the One, some look at Him in a very exclusive way and think that the God they worship is the only One, and there are others who see Him as pervading the entire Creation and worship Him in an inclusive way.

This pluralistic approach is necessary to maintain harmony in a world with people of diverse beliefs. Respect for the belief of others is an essential characteristic of the Hindu philosophy of life as expressed in the Gita.

19) I give heat, I withhold and send forth the rain; I am immortality and death; I am being as well as non-being, O Arjuna.

Comment: Here the Lord declares Himself in totality as the Source and Nourisher of the whole of Creation. In such a grand expression, He reveals to Arjuna that immortality and death also – two apparently divergent states – are harmonized in Him. The relationship between immortality and death is like substance and its shadow.

20) The knowers of the three Vedas, the drinkers of Soma, purified from sin, worship Me by sacrifices and pray for the way to heaven. They reach the holy world of the Lord of the Devas and enjoy in heaven the celestial pleasures of the Devas.

21) After enjoying the vast heavenly world, they return to the world of mortals when the merits, that they achieved, become exhausted. Thus, following the injunctions of the three Vedas in striving to satisfy the objects of desires, they go and come.

22) To those men who worship Me alone, thinking of no other and who are ever devout, I provide for their gain and security.

23) Even those devotees who are full of Shraddha and worship other gods, they actually worship Me alone, O son of Kunti, although by the wrong method.

24) I am verily the Enjoyer and the Lord of all Yajnas, but these men do not know Me in reality; hence they descend.

> *Comment 20-24: Those who worship in an exclusive way pray for the enjoyment of finite objects and go after death to a heavenly world for the satisfaction of their pleasure, but they return again to the mortal world when their merits have been exhausted.*
>
> *Indeed the Lord provides prosperity and protection to those who worship Him.*
>
> *These men who worship god in an exclusive way do not realise that there is an Over-Lord who receives all their offerings and, as a result of wrong understanding, they do not reach the final Abode.*

25) Votaries of the Devas go to the Devas; the votaries of the Pitrus go to the Pitrus; to the Bhutas go to the Bhuta worshippers; My devotees come to Me.

26) Whoever offers to Me with devotion a leaf, a flower, a fruit or a drop of water, I accept that offering which has come from a pure and pious heart.

> *Comment 25-26: Whatever one prays for, one gets. Therefore it is important that one should have the understanding to pray for that, which by getting gives eternal satisfaction. But most people are short-sighted and pray only for finite things. These things may give great pleasure, but when the merit on which they depend expires, one returns back to earth to start all over again. Therefore, rather than worshiping for pleasurable things, one should worship the Lord for His own sake. Elaborate rituals are not necessary. What is important is simple devotion and sincerity of heart. The Lord responses to the prayer of all, but those who make simple offerings with a pure resolve are considered dearest to Him.*

27) Whatever you do, whatever you eat, whatever you offer in sacrifice, whatever gift you make, whatever austerity you practise, O Kaunteya, let all be as an offering to Me.

28) By so doing you will be free from the bondage of actions that yield good and bad results. With the mind firmly set in practising the Yoga of Renunciation and liberated, you shall come to Me.

> *Comment 27-28: Remembering the Lord is the most vital thing of life. The Lord again stresses the importance of remembering Him at all times. Only those moments that we remember Him are Real Life. The other part is like wasting of life. It is not easy to think of Him all the time without some adjustment. One way of doing it is to offer whatever we do, what we give and whatever we get to the Divine. By so doing the mind becomes focused and awareness of the Presence of the Lord gradually becomes natural. As a result of the spirit of detachment, one will attain to the glory of the Lord and have eternal satisfaction.*

29) I am the same to all beings; to Me there is none hateful, none dear. But those who worship Me with devotion, they are in Me and I am also in them.

30) Even if a man of the most sinful conduct worships Me with undeviating devotion, he must be considered as righteous, for he has made the right resolve.

31) Soon does he become a man of righteousness and obtains lasting peace. O Kaunteya, know for certain that My devotee never perishes.

> *Comment 29-31: The Lord does not make any distinction between one person and another. Everything depends on the person. If he is devoted, by virtue of that devotion he establishes an intimate relationship with the Lord. Since he thinks all the time of the Lord and depends solely on Him, the Lord becomes*

like his Home in which he lives. By thinking of the Lord constantly also causes Him to be in his mind.

An example may be given of the sun shining in pots of water. The pots are in the sunshine and the reflection of the sun is also in the pots of water.

There is a story of a blind saint who was singing and travelling by foot to Vrindaban. At midday he was very hungry and thirsty. A little boy came to him with some food. He said to the saint: "My mother has sent this food for you. Come in the shade and eat it." The saint said: "Look, my child, I am blind. How do I know where to find a shade? Take my hand and lead me to it." When the boy stretched out his little hand, the saint grabbed it. The boy was screaming, "Let go. You are hurting my hand!" Said the saint: "I am not going to let you go. I have been searching for you all my life." The saint knew that the voice was no ordinary human voice. It was the Divine voice of his Lord Krishna. When he eventually let Him go, he said to Him: "You have escaped from my hand but do You think you can escape from my heart?"

Therefore, personal effort is considered the most important thing. If we take one step towards the Lord, He makes a hundred steps towards us. This is sadhana. It is not something one practises at convenience. It calls for determined effort, for sacrifice.

Another story is about Narad Muni. One day he happened to enter a temple where everyone was singing the glory of the Lord. "We really want to see You, Lord. Come to us, O Lord, we really want to see You." They were singing with so much devotion that tears were flowing from their eyes. Narad was full of compassion for them. Immediately he went to Vaikuntha, the Abode of the Lord, and said: "My Lord, You are known to be very compassionate to Your devotees. Why don't you respond to those devotees who are crying their hearts out? It appears to me that You are very callous!" The Lord said, "Narad! Are you sure those devotees truly want to see Me?" Narad: "Yes my Lord. Yes my Lord. They are dying to see You!" The Lord went with Narad and suddenly He stopped. Narad said, "Come my Lord, only four more villages to go." The Lord said, "Narad! Go and call the devotees." Narad: "Let us go, my Lord. Only four villages more." The Lord said, "Narad! I have come all the way from Vaikuntha. Can't these devotees come when I am only four villages away?"

Narad saw the logic. He went and when the devotees saw him again they were very happy. Narad said, "I have good news for you. I have very good news for you. The Lord has come to give you 'darshan' (blessing)." Everyone was full of jubilation. "Where is the Lord? Where is the Lord?" they asked. "Only four villages from here. Let us go", Narad replied. With great zest everyone got up. But before they started, some began to complain and make excuses. Some asked, "But why didn't the Lord come here?" Some others said that it was already too late and that it was time for them to go home! However, some devotees went on their way to meet the Lord, but before they could reach where the Lord was, there was one excuse after the other. In the end, only one person turned up where the Lord was. With an amusing smile on His lips the Lord asked, "Where are all the devotees, Narad?" Narad could not raise his head. Only one devotee reached the Lord Who embraced him and showered him with blessings.

One must never judge a person. Even the most sinful person can be transformed by being devoted and following correct instructions. And when that happens, he enjoys everlasting peace. The temptations of the world no longer affect him. Temptations deprive us of our sense of dispassion and our willpower, and we get drowned in the ocean of delusion.

An example is Valmiki who was evil but by constantly repeating the holy name of the Lord, he was transformed into a saint. He was the author of the great Ramayana, the life story of Lord Rama.

32) For those who take refuge in Me, O Partha, though they are of humble birth – women, traders and labourers – even they attain the Supreme Goal.

33) How much more then the holy Brahmanas and devoted, royal saints! Having come into this transient, joyless world, do worship Me.

34) Fix your mind on Me; be devoted to Me; sacrifice unto Me; bow down to Me. With yourself made steadfast in Me and taking Me as the Supreme Goal, you will come to Me.

Comment 32-34: The Lord is not partial or impartial. He does not consider the status of anyone and does not reject anyone. Even Sabari, who belonged to the Bhil tribe, received His gracious blessings. Then why not others who are fortunate to be born royal or well-learned. The important thing is to realise how impermanent are the things of the world and to surrender to the Lord, recognizing Him as the ultimate Goal of life. Unfortunately, with power and high status some tend to think that they are well secured until problems start. They treat the humble with disdain not knowing that the Lord dwells equally in all. The Lord sets an example of recognizing the worth of all and no one is too sinful to receive His grace.

CHAPTER TEN:

The Yoga of Divine Manifestations

1) The Blessed Lord said: O mighty-armed one, listen to My supreme word. Out of desire to do you good, I wish to speak of it to your absorbing delight.

> *Comment: So far the Lord has been giving Arjuna extremely good teachings, but He now says that for his greatest good He is going to teach him that which is most Supreme, and for which he would find a natural attraction. The message of this opening verse will certainly grip the attention of Arjuna who has been listening keenly to the Lord's words.*

2) Neither the hosts of Devas nor the great Rishis know My origin; for in every respect I am the Source of the Devas and the great Rishis.

3) He who knows Me as unborn and without beginning, and as the Great Lord of the worlds, he among mortals is undeluded and freed from all sins.

> *Comment: Indeed, the Lord is giving the most profound teaching. Even the celestial divinities, nor the wise Rishis, are aware of His origin because He is the Source of them all. When one realises that He is without beginning and the Supporter of all the worlds, one becomes free from all impurities.*

4) Intellect, wisdom, non-delusion, patience, truth, self-restraint, calmness, pleasure, pain, birth, death, fear and fearlessness;

The Yoga of Divine Manifestations

5) Non-injury, equanimity, contentment, austerity, charity, fame and infamy – these different qualities of beings come from Me alone.

6) The seven great Rishis and the four ancient Manus, endowed with My power, were born of My mind; and from them have come forth all the creatures in the world.

7) He who knows in truth this glory and power of Mine is gifted with unfaltering yoga; of this there is no doubt.

> *Comment 4-7: The natural characteristics of beings with their modes of conduct, and the first seven Rishis (Sanatkumar and others, who were not born from any womb but are mind-born from the Lord) from whom Creation came into being: the Lord is the Source of them all. Knowing this greatness of the Lord, one becomes steadfast in the practice of yoga and attains the yogic experience of non-separation. With this realization all problems of life are resolved.*

8) I am the Origin of all; from Me all things evolve. The wise know this and adore Me with all their heart.

9) With their minds fixed on Me, with their life absorbed in Me, enlightening one another and speaking of Me always, they are contented and delighted.

10) To those who are ever devout and worship Me with love, I give them the Yoga of Discrimination by which they come to Me.

11) Out of pure compassion for them, dwelling in their hearts, I destroy the ignorance-born darkness by the luminous Lamp of Wisdom.

> *Comment 8-11: Out of love for Arjuna, the Lord declares the great truths about Himself. The wise men, who realise His origin, worship Him with pure devotion and find contentment*

and happiness by singing His glory and discussing amongst themselves His transcendental qualities. He dwells in the hearts of those who worship Him with love and destroy their ignorance by which they are able to make a distinction between the right and the wrong path. And by following the Path of Righteousness they reach the Lord.

12) Arjuna said: You are the Supreme Brahman, the Supreme Abode, the Supreme Purifier, the Eternal, the Divine Purusha, the Primeval Deity, the Unborn and the Omnipresent.

13) All the Rishis, such as Deva Rishi Narada, and also Asita, Devala and Vyasa, have thus acclaimed You. Now You Yourself are saying it to me!

14) I accept all that You have said to me as true. O Kesava! Neither the Devas nor the Danavas really know Your manifestation.

15) Verily, You alone know Yourself by Yourself, O Purushottama, O Source and Lord of beings, God of gods and Ruler of the world.

16) Indeed, only You can tell without reserve Your Divine glories by which You remain pervading all these worlds.

17) O Yogin, how may I know You by constant meditation? O Lord, in what various aspects are You to be thought of by me?

18) Tell Me in detail, O Janardana, of Your yoga powers and attributes, for I am ever eager to hear Your life-infusing words.

Comment 12-18: In the very first verse of this chapter the Lord assured Arjuna that what He was going to teach would be appealing to him. That is exactly what has happened. Arjuna was full of admiration and began to praise the Lord in exalted verbal expressions. Arjuna then asks the Lord how he may have constant awareness of His existence and know His diverse manifestations. He is so inspired by what the Lord has said that he is eager to know about them in detail.

Indirectly, what Arjuna is asking is of value to all of us since we need to understand that the Divine pervades the entire Universe in diverse forms. This understanding is necessary to develop a reverential attitude to all forms of life. This has been nurtured into the psyche of the Hindus for many millenniums through their various scriptures. In fact, it is a unique feature of Hinduism. That is one of the reasons why Hindus worship nature in its varied appearances. Alternative to that is the exploitation of nature with its negative consequences, and also the conflicts and suffering that we witness in the world.

19) The Blessed Lord said: Very well! I shall now tell you My Divine glories according to their prominence, O best of the Kurus. There is no end to the details of My manifestation.

20) I am the Self, O Gudakesa, seated in the hearts of all beings. I am the beginning, the middle and also the end of all beings.

Comment 19-20: The Lord is all-pervasive and therefore, in reality, there can never be an adequate description of Him. But there are aspects that are grander than others and He shall speak of those. One of the recurring teachings of the Gita is that the Lord is without beginning and end. He also dwells in the heart of everyone. When the Lord dwells in the hearts of all, what other grace is required? The Giver within is always showering His Grace like the sun that shines, but we have to open the curtains (remove the illusion) so that it can enter our consciousness. And when we realise the Lord within, then, how can one hate or cause another to hate?

21) Of the Adityas I am Vishnu; of the luminaries I am the radiant Sun; I am Marichi of the Maruts; of the asterisms the Moon am I.

22) Of the Vedas I am the Saman; I am Vasava (Indra) among the Devas; of the senses I am the mind, and among living beings I am consciousness.

23) Of the Rudras I am Sankara, of the Yakshas and Rakshasas I am Kubera. Of the Vasus I am Pavaka and of mountains I am Meru.

24) Of priests, O Partha, know Me to be the chief, Brihaspati; of generals I am Skanda and of bodies of water I am the ocean.

25) Of the great Rishis I am Bhrigu; of utterances I am the monosyllable 'Om'. Of Yajnas I am Japayajna, and of unmoving things the Himalaya.

26) Of all trees I am Asvattha; of Deva Rishis I am Narada; of the Gandharvas I am Chitraratha and of the Siddhas I am the Muni Kapila.

27) Of horses, know Me to be the nectar-born Ucchaisravas; of lordly elephants, Airavata and of men, the monarch.

28) Of weapons I am the thunderbolt; of cows I am Kamadhuk; I am Kandarpa of the progenitors; of serpents I am Vasuki.

29) Of the Nagas I am Ananta; of the water-deities I am Varuna. Of the Pitrus I am Aryama; of controllers I am Yama.

30) Of the Daityas I am Prahlada and of reckoners I am Time; of beasts I am the lord of beasts (lion), and Vainateya (Garuda) of birds.

31) Of purifiers I am the wind; of the wielders of weapon I am Rama. Of fishes I am the shark, and of rivers I am the Ganges.

32) Of created things I am the beginning and the end and also the middle, O Arjuna. Of the sciences I am the science of the Self; of those who debate I am reason.

33) Of letters I am the letter A, and of word-compounds I am the Dual (Dvandva). I am verily the eternal Time. I am the Dispenser facing everywhere.

34) And I am the all-devouring Death. I am the prosperity of those who are prosperous; and of female qualities I am Fame, Fortune, Speech, Memory, Intelligence, Constancy and Forbearance.

35) Of the Saman hymns I am the Brihat-Saman; of metres I am Gayatri. Of months I am Margasirsha and of seasons I am the flowery spring.

36) I am the gambling of the fraudulent. I am the splendour of the splendid; I am victory; I am effort; I am the goodness of the good.

37) Of the Vrishnis I am Vasudeva; of the Pandavas I am Dhananjaya; of the sages I am Vyasa and of the seers I am Usana the seer.

38) Of punishers I am the scepter; of those that seek victory I am statesmanship; and of secrets I am also silence; and I am the wisdom of the wise.

39) And whatever is the seed of all beings, that am I, O Arjuna. There is no being, whether moving or unmoving that can exist without Me.

40) There is no end of My Divine manifestations, O harasser of foes; know this to be only a brief exposition of the extent of My glories.

41) Whatever being there is glorious, prosperous or powerful, know that to have sprung but from a spark of My splendour.

42) But what need is there, O Arjuna, for this detailed knowledge?

I stand supporting the whole Universe with a single atom of Myself.

Comment 21-42: The Lord gives a brief and illuminating description of the prominent aspects of His manifestations which are to be known by scientific and intellectual enquiry. This understanding ultimately leads to the Lord in His unmanifest form. As the Vedas say: relativity itself presupposes an Absolute. This is the highest teaching any religion can offer. It is essential for us to understand that Lord Krishna is asking us to investigate, and not to accept merely on faith. This is the greatness of the teachings of the Gita.

Among the important things memory is mentioned. According to science, after every period of seven years all the old molecules of the human body are replaced by new ones. But unless there is something constant, it is not possible to remember things that happen before seven years. There are people who even remember events of previous lives: how do we account for that? Elsewhere, the Lord says that He is the Unchangeable in the bodies that are changeable and that He is memory.

It was necessary for the Lord to explain to Arjuna that what He had recounted to him was just a brief description of His prominence, and they were only tiny sparks of what He is. In reality, the whole Universe is supported by a single atom of Himself.

If the Universe is supported by a single atom of the Lord, then there must be innumerable Universes. And as the Vedas declared, whatever we know of the Absolute, a part will always remain unknown until we have full realization. The time scale and vastness of the Universe are only now being discovered by scientific method and is proving what was known to the Hindus thousands of years ago. This may appear to be a mystery but we cannot ignore the facts. The probability is that the ancient people were more advanced in scientific knowledge than we credit them for.

CHAPTER ELEVEN

THE YOGA OF UNIVERSAL REVELATION

Arjuna said:

1) By this profound discourse concerning the Self, which You have delivered out of compassion for me, my delusion has been dispelled.

2) I have heard from You, O lotus-eyed One, in detail of the origin and dissolution of beings and also of Your inexhaustible greatness.

3) As You have declared Yourself to be, so it is, O Lord Supreme. (Yet) I desire to see Your Ishwara form, O Purushottama.

4) O Lord, if You think it is possible for me to see it, then do, O Lord of Yoga, show me Your Eternal Self.

> *Comment 1-4: Earlier, Arjuna raised some objections for engaging in the battle with the Kauravas and came to the conclusion that it would be better to live on alms. Krishna then gave him reasons for fighting. Now Arjuna is saying that – as a result of what He had said – the confusion which he had has been cleared. He is convinced about whatever Krishna says about Himself and expressed the desire to see the Supreme Form of the Lord. He was asking for something unimaginable, something that was never witnessed before. Quite naturally, even though the Lord had said He was the All-Powerful, there were some doubts in Arjuna's mind, and he implores the Lord to reveal His supreme form if that were possible!*

5) The Blessed Lord said: Behold My forms, O Partha, by hundreds and thousands, manifold and Divine and of multi-colours and shapes.

6) Behold the Adityas, the Vasus, the Rudras, the two Aswins and also the Maruts. Behold, O Bharata, many marvels that were never seen before.

7) Behold here today, O Gudakesa, the whole Universe of the moving and the unmoving, and whatever else you desire to see – see all of them as integral parts of My body.

> *Comment 5-7: What a wonderful day it is! The Lord is eager to dispel all the doubts of His friend and spoke to him as if he were asking for a very simple thing!*
>
> *He tells Arjuna to look in His supra-cosmic form and there he will see everything that exists in the Universe and even other unknown things as well!*
>
> *The Adityas, Vasus, Rudras, Aswins and Maruts are all different names mentioned in the Vedas of the same Absolute (ekam Sat) and when worship is done with that understanding then the fruit of worship is of a permanent nature.*

8) But you cannot see Me with these natural eyes of yours; I give you Divine sight; behold My Supreme Yoga.

> *Comment: The Lord explains to Arjuna that the human lens of the eyes do not have the capacity to visualize that Supra-Cosmic Form. He needs another pair of lenses! He has to have a celestial pair which the Lord has decided to furnish.*

9) Sanjaya said: Having spoken thus, O King, the great Lord of Yoga, Hari, revealed to Partha His supreme Iswara form.

10) With many mouths and eyes, with many marvellous sights,

The Yoga of Universal Revelation

with many Divine ornaments, with many uplifted Divine weapons;

11) Wearing heavenly garments and raiments, anointed with celestial perfumes, all wonderful, resplendent, boundless, with faces on all sides.

12) If the splendour of a thousand suns were to blaze forth all at once in the sky, that would somewhat be like the splendour of that Mahatman.

13) There in the body of the God of gods, Pandava then saw the whole Universe with its many divisions drawn together into one.

14) Then Dhananjaya was struck with amazement. With his hair standing on end, he bowed his head to the Lord in adoration and spoke with joined palms.

> *Comment 9-14: How privileged is Sanjaya! He seems to have been gifted with Divine eyes to see exactly what Arjuna is witnessing. Arjuna is not the only person to behold this Majestic form of the Lord. Sanjaya's words are telling and his description is exceptional. It is better not to attempt a comment on them. Let the reader read those words again, contemplate on them and try to visualize his masterly description!*

15) Arjuna said: I see all the gods, O God, in Your body, and hosts of all grades of beings: Brahma, the Lord, seated on the lotus and all the Rishis and celestial serpents.

16) I behold You, infinite in forms on all sides, with countless arms, stomachs, mouths and eyes; neither Your end nor the middle nor the beginning do I see, O Lord of the Universe, O Universal form.

17) I see You with diadem, club, and discus; a mass of radiance blazing everywhere, hard to look at, all round dazzling like flaming fire and sun, and immeasurable.

18) You are the Imperishable, the Supreme Being to be realised. You are the great Treasure-house of this Universe; You are the Imperishable Guardian of the Eternal Dharma. You are the ancient Purusha, I deem.

> Comment 15-18: *Arjuna expresses his admiration of what he sees of the varied aspects of the Lord, realizing that everything exists within Him. For the humans living in the world and indeed for all Creation, He has made an Eternal Law or Sanatana Dharma. This is not man-made. It already existed before human beings came on this planet. It co-existed with Creation and sustains it. That Law is indispensable, and the Lord Himself protects it so that it can operate for the good of the world. And elsewhere, He said that He comes into this world from time to time to protect it.*

19) I see You without beginning, middle or end, infinite in power, of infinite arms, the sun and the moon being Your eyes, the burning fire in Your mouth, heating the whole Universe with Your radiance.

20) This space between heaven and earth and all the quarters are filled by You alone. Having seen this, Your marvellous and terrible form, the three worlds are trembling with fear, O Mahatman.

21) These hosts of Devas indeed enter into You; some in awe extol You with joined palms; bands of great Rishis and Siddhas pronounce: "May it be well", and praise You with sublime hymns.

22) The Rudras, Adityas, Vasus, Sadhyas, Viswas, Asvins, Maruts, Ushmapas, hosts of Gandharvas, Yakshas, Asuras and Siddhas – they are all gazing at You, and they are amazed.

> Comment 19-22: *The Lord reveals Himself to satisfy Arjuna, His friend and devotee, but in so doing so many other beings benefit. From the good work of one man so many people reap the fruits; even so with the work of an evil man so many are*

affected by the consequences. That is why Law is necessary. Without Law everyone is left unprotected. Dharma is the Primary Law – the Law of Coexistence – and all other man-made laws are also meant for a similar purpose. And when the man-made laws become outdated due to a greater understanding or changed circumstances, they are either withdrawn or adapted to meet new situations.

The Rudras and Adityas, etc., are Vedic deities whose roles are to maintain the functioning of the sacred Law. They are 33 altogether. In reality, they represent different functions of the same Absolute. But like Arjuna, they too, like waves in the ocean, are subject to Cosmic Law at a higher plane of existence.

23) Seeing Your immeasurable form with innumerable mouths, and eyes, arms, thighs and feet, stomachs and terrible tusks – the worlds are terror-struck, and so am I.

24) When I look at You touching the sky, blazing with many colours, wide open mouths and large fiery eyes, my heart trembles in fear and I find neither courage nor peace, O Vishnu!

25) When I see Your mouths terrible with tusks resembling fires of universal destruction, I do not find peace. Be gracious, O Lord of the gods, O Abode of the Universe.

26-27) All the sons of Dhritarastra with hosts of kings of the earth, Bhishma, Drona, Sutaputra, with the warrior chiefs of ours, briskly entering Your mouth, terrible with tusks and fearful to look at. Some are found sticking in the gaps between the teeth with their heads crushed into powder.

28) Truly, as the many torrents of rivers rush towards the ocean, so do these heroes in the world of men throw themselves into Your fiercely flaming mouths.

29) As moths rush headlong into a blazing fire for destruction, so

do these creatures hurriedly speed into Your mouths for their own destruction.

30) Devouring all the worlds on every side with Your flaming mouths, You lick Your lips. Your fiery rays that fill the whole world with radiance, are burning, O Vishnu!

31) Tell me who You are, so fierce in form. I bow down to You, O God Supreme; have mercy. I desire to know You, the Primal One. I know not Your purpose.

32) The Blessed Lord said: I am the mighty world-destroying Time, now engaged in wiping out the world. Even without you the warriors arrayed in hostile armies shall not live.

33) You, therefore, arise and obtain fame. Conquer the enemies and enjoy the unrivalled kingdom. By Me they have verily been slain already. You merely be an outward cause, O Savyasachin.

34) Slay Drona, Bhishma, Jayadratha, Karna and other brave warriors, who are already doomed by Me. Be not distressed with fear. Fight and you will conquer your enemies in battle.

> *Comment 23-34: Arjuna first saw the benign aspect of the Lord. Now he sees His dreadful aspect: the realistic nature of life, governed by Maha Kaal. Time is the great eater of everything. Within it functions the Law of Decay from which nothing can escape. No one likes this aspect. It is terrifying, but it is all part of the process of Creation. The Lord assured him that this world is merely a stage and he is only an actor in the hands of the Director. The drama will go on even without him. Therefore, he should not be too anxious as if he were a free agent! The fate of those who have violated the Immortal Dharma has already been sealed by their own action. He is merely an instrument.*

35) Sanjaya said: Having heard that speech of Kesava, the crowned

The Yoga of Universal Revelation

one (Arjuna) with joined palms, trembling and overwhelmed with fear, prostrated himself and addressed Krishna in a choked voice.

> *Comment: When Arjuna saw this terrible aspect of the Lord and heard what He said, he was afraid of the consequences that would befall the world. He was so overwhelmed that he prostrated in front of the Lord and spoke in a voice full of emotion.*

36) Arjuna said: O Hrishikesa! It is only natural that the world is delighted and rejoices in Your praise while the Rakshasas fly in fear in all directions, and all the hosts of Siddhas bow to You.

37) And why should they not bow to You, O great-souled One Who is greater (than all) and is the Primal Cause of even Brahma, O Infinite Being, O Lord of gods, O Abode of the Universe? You are the Imperishable, the being and the non-being and that which is the Supreme.

38) You are the Primal God, the Ancient Purusha; You are the Supreme Abode of all this. You are the Knower and the knowable. You, O Being of infinite form, pervade this entire Universe.

39) You are Vayu, Yama, Agni, Varuna, the Moon, Prajapati and the Great-grandfather. Salutation to You a thousand times, again and again salutation to You.

40) Salutation to You from the front, salutation to You from behind, salutation to You on every side, O All! Infinite in might and immeasurable in strength, You pervade all and therefore You are all.

41) Whatever I have rashly said out of carelessness or love, addressing You as "O Krishna, O Yadava, O friend," looking on You merely as a friend, ignorant of Your greatness;

42) In whatever way I may have insulted You in joke while at

play, reposing, sitting or at meals, when alone, O Achyuta, or in company — that I implore You, Immeasurable One, to forgive.

43) You are the Father of this world, everything that is moving or unmoving. You are to be adored by this world. You are the Greatest Guru. None exists who is equal to You in the three worlds. Who then can excel You, O Being of unequalled power?

44) Therefore, bowing down and prostrating my body, I implore You, adorable Lord to forgive me. Bear with me, O Lord, as a father with his son, as a friend with a friend, as a lover with his beloved.

45-46) I rejoice that I have seen what was never seen before, but my mind is puzzled and in fear. I desire to see You as before, in your former form having four arms, crowned, bearing a mace and a discus in Your hands, O thousand-armed, O Universal Form.

> *Comment 36-46: After realizing Who Krishna really is, Arjuna begins to glorify Him and repents that he did not know Him as the Supreme before. He begs the Lord to forgive him for the way he had treated Him and to be indulgent with Him just as a friend will be with another friend or a lover with his beloved. This is the positive side of the human emotion. Forgiveness is not very emphatic in Hinduism.*

> *The Law of Karma is. But here, it is not a case of transgression knowingly as we find in case of Shishupala who was forgiven a hundred times, but ultimate killed by Krishna because his wrongdoings were deliberate. The impact of karma is terrible when it is done in a calculating manner. The fate of the Kauravas was sealed because of their evil deeds.*

47) The Blessed Lord said: Graciously, I have revealed to you by My yoga power, O Arjuna, this resplendent, universal, infinite, primeval, supreme form, which none else has ever seen but you.

> *Comment: The Lord sees Arjuna as spiritually fit to benefit*

The Yoga of Universal Revelation

from that Supreme Revelation. But even then he needed something more which he could not achieve on his own. That was supplemented by the 'divya chakshu' (divine eye) provided by the Lord. Arjuna's innocence won him this great favour.

48) Not by study of the scriptures, nor by sacrifices, nor by charity, nor by rituals, nor by severe austerity, can this form of Mine be seen in the world of men by any one else but you, O hero of the Kurus.

49) Be neither afraid nor bewildered on seeing this terrific form of Mine; free from fear and delighted at heart, see again My former form.

50) Sanjaya said: Having spoken thus to Arjuna, Vasudeva showed again His own form; and assuming His gentle form consoled him who was terrified.

51) Arjuna said: Seeing Your gentle human form, O Janardana, I am now composed and restored to my normal self.

52) The Blessed Lord said: This form of Mine, which you have seen, is very difficult indeed to see. Even the Devas are very eager to see it.

53) Neither by study of the Scriptures, nor by the practice of austerities, nor by charity, nor by sacrifice can I be seen in this form as you have seen Me.

54) But by unswerving devotion this form can be known, seen in reality and entered into, O scorcher of foes.

55) He who does work for Me, looks on Me as the Supreme, is devoted to Me, is free from attachment, and is without hatred for any being, he comes to Me, O Pandava.

Comment 48-55: The Lord consoles Arjuna and tells him

that the revelation that he witnessed has not been seen before by anyone. Even though there are other spiritual practitioners who are all doing well, this form of the Lord can only be seen through steadfast devotion. Devotion here does not mean only chanting and worshiping, but also doing seva and being free from attachment and hatred towards all beings. All others are also dear to the Lord, but these devoted ones are particularly dear to Him because they are not only practising for their own benefit, but they are of value for the entire Creation. This special favour was done to Arjuna for the good of humankind.

In the Devi Sukta of the Rigveda is mentioned the Cosmic realization of Vak Rishi. Vak Rishi saw the Cosmic form, inclusive of all the deities. The difference, however, is that one is Realization and the other is Revelation. Realization is open to all but Revelation depends on special favour and grace of the Lord.

CHAPTER TWELVE

THE YOGA OF DEVOTION

1) Arjuna said: Those devotees who steadfastly worship You and those again who worship the Imperishable or the Unmanifest – which of these are better qualified in the practice of yoga?

> *Comment: This question is being asked even today when some think that worshiping the Lord as Unmanifest is more important than the Personal aspect. Arjuna wants to know which of the two should be considered as greater.*

2) The Blessed Lord said: I consider those perfect in yoga who have fixed their minds on Me and endowed with supreme Shraddha, worship Me steadfastly.

3) But those who worship the Imperishable, the Indefinable, the Unmanifest, the Omnipresent, the Unthinkable, the Unchangeable, the Immovable and the Eternal –

4) Having restrained all their senses, even-minded everywhere and engaged in the welfare of all beings – verily they also come to Me.

5) Greater is their difficulty who worship the Unmanifest, for the goal of the Unmanifest is very hard for the embodied beings to reach.

> *Comment 2-5: The Lord says that those who worship the Personal and those who worship the Impersonal, both reach*

the same Goal. But it is more difficult for those who worship the Impersonal to fix their minds on the formless. Their sadhana lies in the practice of self-control and seva (selfless service) to all beings. Their devotion is centred on what they are doing and as a result they become detached from the sense of belonging and possession. To them the whole world is one family. When one works for the family one does not think of personal rewards.

6) But those who worship Me, renouncing all actions in Me, regarding Me as the Supreme Goal, meditating on Me with single-minded yoga –

7) For them who set their thought on Me, I become very soon, O Partha, the deliverer from the ocean of the mortal Samsara.

Comment 6-7: Those who worship the Personal must also perform actions but they must dedicate everything to the Lord by thinking of Him always while acting. By so doing their minds become fixed on Him by Whose Grace they are liberated from birth and death.

8) Fix your mind on Me alone, let your thoughts dwell on Me. You will hereafter live in Me alone. Of this there is no doubt.

9) If you are not able to this, O Dhananjaya, then seek to reach Me by Abhyasa-yoga.

10) If you are unable even to practise Abhyasa-yoga, be you intent on doing work for My sake; by performing actions for My sake only you will attain perfection.

11) If you are not able even to do this, then taking refuge in Me, abandon the fruits of all actions with the self subdued.

12) Better indeed is knowledge than (formal) Abhyasa; better than knowledge is meditation; better than meditation is the

renunciation of the fruit of action; peace immediately follows renunciation.

> *Comment 8-12: Alternative ways are prescribed through which one can reach the Goal. This pluralistic approach is an expression of a liberal attitude. In it there is room for discussion – to look at things more philosophically. While the Lord deems all the paths as equally important, the emphasis is on Karma Yoga because only by serving the entire Creation there can be peace.*
>
> *Dwelling on the thoughts of the Lord gradually leads to being conscious of His Presence. To engage in the service of Creation means also serving the Lord, who dwells in all beings, and this is pleasing to Him.*
>
> *Without freedom and the spirit of enquiry one cannot discover the truth. Religion should encourage the search for truth and not become dogmatic which is opposed to this enquiry. As a result there is stagnation and blind faith, which religious leaders may take advantage of for their own benefit.*
>
> *It is to the credit of the Hindu religion that it is not afraid to encourage questions. In this spirit lies its real strength. Throughout its history, from the Vedas to the Gita, this outlook prevails, which gives it a universal vision and makes it responsive to scientific discoveries.*

13) He who hates no being, who is friendly and compassionate to all, who is free from the feeling of 'I and mine', even-minded in pain and pleasure and forbearing,

14) Always content, steadfast in meditation, self-controlled and with firm conviction, with mind and intellect fixed on Me, he – My devotee – is dear to Me.

15) He who does not cause problems to the world and the world

is not a problem to him, he who is free from joy, anger, fear and anxiety – he is dear to Me.

16) He who has no wants, is pure, prompt, unconcerned, untroubled, who is selfless in all his activities, and is thus devoted to Me, is dear to Me.

17) That person is dear to Me who neither rejoices nor hates anyone, who grieves not nor has any desires; who has renounced good and evil and is full of devotion.

18) He who has equal regards for foe and friend and is the same in honour and dishonour, who is the same in cold and heat, in pleasure and pain, who is free from attachment;

19) To whom censure and praise are equal, is silent, content with anything, homeless, steady-minded, full of devotion – that person is dear to Me.

20) They, who devotedly follow this immortal Dharma as described above and endued with Shraddha, looking upon Me as the Supreme Goal, and devoted – they are exceedingly dear to Me.

> *Comment 17-20: These verses consist of the essential message of the Gita. The Lord Himself terms them as the Sanatana Dharma – eternal religion. It is applicable at all times, at all places and for all mankind. All other values of religion may change but these do not, because they are the sustaining principles of life.*
>
> *The teaching is not to hate any being, to be friendly and compassionate to all, to be always contented, not to cause any problem to the world, to be free from all wants, to be the same to friend and foe and take insult and praise in the same spirit. Those who follow this teaching are exceedingly dear to God. One may follow other kinds of teaching that may please God.*

But anyone who violates those teachings expressed above and believes that He will be pleased by the wholesale slaughtering of His Creation in His name is anti-God. That is the implication.

CHAPTER THIRTEEN

THE YOGA OF DISCRIMINATION BETWEEN THE FIELD AND ITS KNOWER

1) The Blessed Lord said: This body, O Kaunteya, is known as the Kshetra (the field) and the sages call him who knows it as Kshetrajna.

2) Know Me as the Kshetrajna in all Kshetras, O Bharata. The knowledge of both the Kshetra and Kshetrajna is deemed by Me as perfect knowledge.

> *Comment 1-2: The Lord explains that this has already been discussed by the ancient sages and to view the scientific knowledge together with knowledge of the Self as complete knowledge! One is subjective (analytical), the other is objective (investigative). The subjective science is considered to be superior because it gets rid of grief. Material science gives physical comfort. In the pursuit of both the greatest good is achieved.*

3) Hear from Me briefly what the Kshetra is and what its properties are. What are its modifications, what is its source, and who He is and what His powers are.

4) This has been sung by the Rishis in many ways, in various distinctive chants and passages that are indicative of Brahman. They are all full of reasoning and convincing.

> *Comment 3-4: Krishna tells Arjuna that He is going to explain to him the properties that go to make up the human*

body, how the body functions and how it changes, its origin and composition, the Divine who sustains it and His powers. These headings completely cover the make up of the human body in its gross and subtle aspects. They have been logically discussed by the ancient Rishis, hence they are very convincing.

Here we have both sciences combined – the physical and the metaphysical. It is necessary to understand that this enlightened philosophical premise was established at the very beginning of the Vedic tradition, and as a result of the freedom of thinking it developed, and in time became a vital part of the culture.

5) They are the great elements, egoism, intellect, as also the unmanifested, the ten organs of perception and action and the mind, and the five objects of the senses;

Comment: The great elements are fire, water, earth, air and ether. These are the primal elements that make up the whole Universe. The ego is primarily the cause of attachment and rebirths, and therefore the objective of Hindu religious practices is to control it and ultimately become liberated from it. The intellect is the guiding principle that distinguishes between what is good and what is harmful. The unmanifest is primal matter, the source of all other categories. The tongue, hands and feet, the generative organ and the organ of defecation are the five organs of action. The five senses are hearing, touch, smell, sight and taste. Each of the five senses has its respective object which attracts it. They are the primal elements – ether, air, earth, fire and water. This research into the constituent human being is unparalleled in the history of ancient world-cultures. As a result, man is looked upon as a responsible being that can plan and shape his future and not a helpless creature. This understanding is necessary for Self-development (yoga).

6) Desire, hatred, pleasure, pain, the aggregate, intelligence, firmness – the Kshetra has been thus briefly described with its modifications.

Comment: The above is not a full description of the field. It is just notes for further discussion. It implies a deeper knowledge and understanding of the physical body and its functioning. Added to it are desire, hatred and pain, which are emotional states of being made up of subtler elements. The aggregate refers to the physical body which consists of the gross elements. Intelligence and steadfastness to higher principles are more positive states that reflect the nature of the Atman or higher Self.

7) Humility, modesty, non-injury, forbearance, uprightness, service of the teacher, purity, steadfastness, self-control;

8) Dispassion towards the objects of the senses, and also absence of egoism; perception of evil in birth, death, old age, sickness and pain;

9) Non-attachment, non-identification of self with son, wife, home, and the like, and constant equanimity in the occurrence of the desirable and the undesirable;

10) Unswerving devotion to Me in the Yoga of Non-separation, resort to secluded places, distaste for the society of men;

11) Constancy in Self-knowledge, perception of the end of the knowledge of Truth; these are declared to be the characteristics of knowledge, and what is opposed to them is ignorance.

Comment 7-11: Religiosity in its truest sense and spiritual knowledge are inseparable. As a person becomes more elevated, the opposites of the above mentioned characteristics become less. Knowledge increases our positiveness in attitude and understanding. On the other hand, ignorance creates misunderstanding and is the basic cause of conflicts. The basis of knowledge is Truth, not dogmas. Ignorance is based on untruth. The untruth may have validity until the Truth is known. After knowing the Truth, if one still rigidly holds on to untruth, it is the sign of stark ignorance.

12) I shall describe to you that which has to be known, and by knowing (that) one attains immortality. Supreme Brahman is without beginning. It is not said to be 'sat' or 'asat'.

> *Comment: After relating the preliminaries, the discussion reaches the point of climax. What is the real purpose of the preliminaries? They are the foundation that has to be properly established in life before the goal can be reached. By practising them, all impurities of the nature are cleansed and Supreme Knowledge is attained. That knowledge which relates to Brahman, the Absolute, leads to immortal life. That Absolute is beyond all genders. It is indescribable. To say It is this or that is being dogmatic. The Vedic doctrine declares It as 'neti neti' (neither this nor that).*

13) With hands and feet everywhere, with eyes and heads and mouths everywhere, with ears everywhere – He exists enveloping all.

14) Shining by the functions of all the senses, yet He is without senses; Absolute, yet sustaining all; devoid of Gunas, yet, He experiences them.

15) Outside and within all beings; the unmoving and also the moving; because of His subtleness He is incomprehensible; He is far yet very near.

16) He is undivided and yet He appears to be divided in beings. He is to be known as the supporter of beings and also as the destroyer and Creator.

17) The Light of all lights, He is said to be beyond darkness; knowledge, the knowable, the goal of knowledge, He is seated in the hearts of all beings.

> *Comment 13-17: Although the Absolute is indescribable yet It can be assumed through Its manifested forms. The above*

verses give a wonderful description of the Divine manifestations of that Absolute and Its all-pervasiveness. Verse 18 sums them up as Light of all lights, seated in the hearts of all beings. Everything that exists has that Divine spark which none can extinguish. All the loud voices of damnation are the mere ranting of the ignorant.

18) Thus the Kshetra (the field), knowledge and That which has to be known, have been briefly described to thee. My devotee, on knowing this, is fitted for My state.

Comment: 'My devotee' means whoever develops those traits as mentioned above that relate to the attainment of knowledge. Knowledge is the great purifier that transforms the sinner into the Divine state of the Lord.

19) Know that Prakriti and Purusha are both without beginning; and know also that all modifications and Gunas are born of Prakriti.

Comment: Scientifically, we cannot attribute a beginning to matter (Prakriti) which is the primal cause of Creation. It is obvious that the diverse Universe with its continuous changes cannot sustain itself. There is a need for a unitary power. Purusha is that unchangeable force which is also without beginning because both originate from the Absolute.

20) Prakriti is said to be the cause by which the body and the senses are created; in the experience of pleasure and pain, Purusha is said to be the cause.

Comment: The body by itself is an inanimate thing. A dead body cannot experience anything. It is the Presence of Purusha, the Divine Life-principle that causes one to experience pleasure and pain through the senses.

21) Purusha, seated in Prakriti, experiences the Gunas born of

Prakriti; attachment to the Gunas is the cause of his birth in good and evil wombs.

> *Comment: In fact it is the Purusha that experiences the modifications that take place in Prakriti (matter) through the Gunas (inherent qualities, causes) in Prakriti. What atoms are to matter, Gunas are to Prakriti. The Gunas are of the nature of Satva, Rajas and Tamas. Satva refers to the neutral force while Tamas and Rajas refer to polarities. According to their different combinations, varieties of forms are created.*

22) The Supreme Purusha in the body is also called the Spectator, the One who permits, the Supporter, the One who experiences, the Great Lord and the Supreme Self.

> *Comment: The position of the Purusha in the body is now defined as the One who witnesses and permits the changes. He is also the Support (like a stage for actors or a screen on which films are projected) on which the changes take place. He is the Spectator (the One who looks at the drama) and who experiences (likes or dislikes of the show). He is also the Great Lord or Master who owns the Field (Prakriti) and who is the Supreme Self that is the Source of all existences. He is independent. All others are dependent.*

23) He who knows the Purusha and Prakriti together with the Gunas is never born again, regardless of what way he may live.

> *Comment: Anyone who experiences the unity of the Lord, the material Universe and Creation, is never born again! It does not matter in what respect he is seen by others! That is why there is no proclamation in Hindu scriptures of false Prophets and no one is persecuted for the beliefs he holds.*

24) By meditation some behold the Self in the self by the Self, others by the Yoga of Knowledge and yet others by the practice of Karma Yoga.

25) Still there are others, not knowing thus, worship as they have heard from others; they too go beyond death by their devotion to what they have heard.

> *Comment 24-25: Human beings are different by nature. In general, some are emotional, some active and some intellectually inclined. Therefore, to suit their different temperaments, different sadhanas (practice) are recommended. This freedom is necessary for spiritual growth and for living peacefully in a world of diverse cultures.*
>
> *The Paths of Meditation, Knowledge and Action are mentioned, but it is admitted that there are others as well which can be learnt from realised persons. These other sources are not looked upon as inferior. The doors to perfection always remain open. The emphasis is on dedication. Unless one is steadfastly dedicated, difficult objectives cannot be achieved.*

26) Whatever being is born, the unmoving or the moving, O best of the Bharatas, know it to be from the union of Kshetra and Kshetrajna.

27) He really sees, who sees the Supreme Lord as the same in all beings, the undying in the dying.

> *Comment 26-27: All creatures whether they are stationary or moving – plants or animals, etc. – are born as a result of the union of Kshetra (the field or Prakriti) and Kshetrajna (the Knower of the field or Purusha).*
>
> *Know him to be a man of realization who sees that the Lord in one being is the same as in all other beings, and within the bodies of the dying is Something that death can never touch.*

28) Because he who sees the Lord, seated the same everywhere, destroys not the Self by the self, therefore he reaches the Supreme Goal.

Comment: The Lord now states the value of such an experience. Since he sees the same Lord within himself as in others, he does not harm himself by harming others. He feels the same pain that he causes to others. Such teaching is necessary to transform the whole world. The Lord is here teaching the unity and interdependence of life. The same body has got different limbs. Whichever limb of the body is affected, the same pain is felt. The man with such experience reaches the Supreme Goal, not others who are still on the path of ignorance, in spite of all their pretensions.

29) He certainly sees who perceives that all actions are done by Prakriti alone and that the Atman is actionless.

Comment: In case we forget, our attention is drawn to the fact that actions are due to the physical aspect of our being. The Atman is the life-force that causes the physical organs as instruments to function.

30) When he realises that the whole variety of beings exists in the One, and is an evolution from that One alone, then he becomes Brahman.

31) This Supreme Self is without beginning, possesses no Gunas and is imperishable. O Kaunteya, though dwelling in the body, It neither acts nor is tainted.

32) As the all-pervading Akasa is not tainted because of its subtlety, so the Self, seated in the body everywhere, is not affected.

33) As the one sun gives radiance to this whole world, so does the Lord of the Kshetra illumine the whole Kshetra, O Bharata.

34) Those who perceive with the eye of wisdom this distinction between the Kshetra and Kshatrajna and the liberation of beings from the Prakriti, they go to the Supreme.

Comment 30-34: The realization that there is a single life-force that animates everything and in which everything exists leaves no room for hatred or malice. As the same sun nourishes everything without any distinction, even so the grace of the Lord reaches everyone. This understanding is necessary to liberate the world from suffering. That knowledge liberates mortals from all suffering.

CHAPTER FOURTEEN:

The Yoga of the three-fold divisions of the Gunas

The Blessed Lord said: I shall again declare that Supreme Knowledge, the best of all forms of knowledge; by knowing which all the sages have proceeded from this world to the highest perfection.

> *Comment: As usual, the Lord starts this chapter also with a stimulating thought. He introduces the subject by revealing that what he is going to deal with is of great importance. The subject-matter is knowledge itself. But this knowledge is greater than all other forms of knowledge dealt with earlier. This knowledge is attained through realization, not revelation. Hence it is attainable by anyone who strives by right means, and it is relevant at all times. The power of this knowledge is that it purifies a person from all sins, and he attains perfection.*

2) Those who devoted themselves to this knowledge and attained unity with Me, are neither born at the time of Creation nor are they disturbed at the time of dissolution.

> *Comment: This knowledge leads to unity with the Lord, whose Abode transcends the worlds which are subjected to the laws of Prakriti. Since they are not born again at the time when the worlds are created, they are not affected at the time of dissolution either. Those who follow that path are free from the natural phenomena with all its upheavals.*

3) My womb is the Mahat Brahma (Prakriti). In that I place the germ. O Bharata, from that all beings are born.

4) O Kaunteya! Whatever forms are produced in any wombs, the great Brahma (Prakriti) is their womb and I am the seed-giving Father.

5) O mighty-armed! The Sattva, Rajas and Tamas Gunas, which are born of Prakriti, bind the indestructible embodied one fast in the body.

> *Comment 3-5: The Lord proceeds to explain the scientific principle of Creation. Prakriti is the material cause and the Lord is the life-bearing principle. As a result of the union of both, beings of different forms are produced. Prakriti consists of three principles known as the Sattva, Rajas and Tamas Gunas. These Gunas are the basic cause for the Divine Sperm to be retained, developed, and progress within the womb (Prakriti) and – even after birth – by attachment to the Gunas.*

6) Of these, Sattva, being pure, is luminous and non-obstructive. It causes bondage, O sinless one, by creating attachment to happiness and attachment to knowledge.

7) Know Rajas to be of the nature of passion, the source of craving and attachment; it binds fast, O Kaunteya, the embodied one by attachment to action.

8) But know Tamas to be born of ignorance. By deluding all embodied beings it binds fast, O Bharata, by heedlessness, indolence and sleep.

> *Comment 6-8: The characteristic of each Guna is being explained in order to understand its functions. Of them Sattva is pure. It is the source of knowledge which removes all problems and leads to happiness. Because Rajas is of the nature of passion,*

> *it is the source of craving. This craving instinct is the cause of attachment.*
>
> *Ignorance is the cause of Tamas. Its characteristic are heedlessness, indolence and sleepy habits.*
>
> *A chain may be made of silver, gold or iron but they all have the capacity to bind. That made of iron (Tamas) may be stronger than the others (Rajas, gold; and Sattva, silver). To be liberated one has to evolve to the weaker link and ultimately transcend them all.*

9) Thus, Sattva binds one to happiness, and Rajas to action, O Bharata, while Tamas indeed binds one to heedlessness by veiling his knowledge.

10) At times Sattva asserts itself, O Bharata, by predominating over Rajas and Tamas; and at other times Rajas dominates over Sattva and Tamas, and in the same way Tamas dominates over Sattva and Rajas.

11) When the light of knowledge gleams through all the gateways of the body, then it may be known that Sattva is predominant.

12) Greed, activity, the undertaking of actions, unrest, longing – these arise, O best of the Bharatas, when Rajas is predominant.

13) Indiscreetness, inertness, heedlessness, and delusion – these arise, O joy of the Kurus, when Tamas is predominant.

> *Comment 9-13: The Gunas are not static. As one predominates over the other, the characteristics and attitudes of an individual changes. An understanding of the functions of the Gunas is necessary to understand the behaviour pattern of an individual. The above verses give an indication of the effects each Guna has on an individual when dominant. Knowing that our character is made up of*

the Gunas, by virtue of that knowledge one can take control of the them and elevate oneself.

14) If the embodied one meets with death when Sattva is predominant, then he goes to the pure worlds of those who perform virtuous deeds.

15) Meeting with death in the Rajas state, he is born among those attached to action; and, dying in Tamas, he is born in the wombs of the deluded.

> Comment 14-15: *The effects of the Gunas on the whole life of an individual from birth to death is summed up. The implication is that all our actions in this life are carried over to the next life. These also decide the position in which an individual will be born. Therefore, by taking care to follow the higher principles of life, one gains in the present and ensures a dignified future life as well.*

16) The fruit of good action, they say, is Sattvika and pure; verily the fruit of Rajas is pain, and ignorance is the fruit of Tamas.

17) From Sattva Guna arises wisdom, and greed from Rajas; heedlessness and error arise from Tamas and also ignorance.

18) Those who are engrossed in Sattva go upwards; the Rajasikas remain in the middle; and the Tamasikas, abiding in the functions of the lowest Guna, go downwards.

> Comment 16-18: *The results from each of the Gunas are presented to highlight the advantages and disadvantages of being attached to one or the other Guna. The Sattvic path leads to knowledge and wisdom which are elevating. The others lead to degeneration and are not encouraged because of their negative results. The idea that is presented here is that there is the possibility of losing this human birth through much indulgence in the Tamasic way of life.*

19) When the seer perceives no other agent than the Gunas, and knows Him who is higher than the Gunas, he enters into My Being.

20) The embodied one attains immortality after being freed from birth, death, decay, pain and these three Gunas, out of which the body is evolved.

> *Comment 16-20: As mentioned earlier, inherent in Prakriti (the material cause of Creation) is the Divine Life Principle. Attachment to the Gunas prevents one from becoming conscious of any other reality than the physical existence what has been evolved from the Gunas. When, by following the Sattvic path, one realises the Lord of the Gunas, then he attains immortal life, being liberated from the dreadful experiences of human life.*

21) Arjuna said: What are the signs of him, O Lord, who has crossed over the three Gunas? What is his conduct? And how does he rise above the Gunas?

> *Comment: Arjuna raises three practical questions that are important to maintain a rational outlook in religion. Such questions are necessary to free religion from its dogmatic posture. How does one know whether a person is saintly? By what signs? Is it by what he says about himself or others say about him, or is it by his conduct? Moreover, is there a system which one can follow in order to transcend the Gunas? These questions are relevant for all times and must be uppermost in the mind of the seeker.*

22) The Blessed Lord said: O Pandava, the person who hates not light, activity and delusion, when present, nor longs after them when absent;

23) He who sits like one unconcerned, is not moved by the Gunas, who knows that the Gunas operate, is firm and moves not;

24) Balanced in pleasure and pain, Self-absorbed, views a clod of earth, a stone and gold alike; the same to agreeable and disagreeable, firm, the same in censure and praise;

25) Who is the same in honour and dishonour, alike to friend and foe, free from all undertakings – he is said to have arisen above the Gunas.

> *Comment 22-25: The Lord describes the characteristics of one who is above the Gunas as one who is liberated from the pairs of opposites. He is also above what is generally understood as 'religiosity'. He is not influenced by worldly values, which are the causes of friendship and enmity and all the conflicts between man and man.*

26) And he who serves Me with unswerving devotion and goes beyond the Gunas, is fitted for becoming Brahman.

27) I am indeed the Abode of Brahman, the Immortal, the Immutable, the Eternal Dharma and Absolute Bliss.

> *Comment 26-27: In conclusion, the achievement of the man who is freed from the Gunas is described as attaining the highest state which is the Abode of the Eternal Dharma and Absolute Bliss. This is the Goal that awaits the man who practises the yogic disciplines of self-control, devotion, service to all beings and compassion.*

CHAPTER FIFTEEN:

THE YOGA OF THE SUPREME SELF

1) The Blessed Lord said: They speak of an imperishable Asvattha-tree which has its roots above and its branches below. Its leaves are the Vedas; he who knows it is truly the knower of the Vedas.

2) Below and above spread its branches, nourished by the Gunas. Sense-objects are its buds and below in the world of men stretch forth its roots that stimulate action.

3) Its form, its end, origin or its existence are not perceived here in this world. After cutting this firm-rooted Asvattha into pieces with the strong axe of non-attachment;

4) Then that Goal should be sought for by going from which they do not return again. I seek refuge in that Primeval Purusha whence streamed forth the Eternal Activity.

> *Comment 1-4: The wise teacher points out to the disciple the obstacles that are in the way and advises him about the means to overcome them. There is a warning that these obstacles are not quite obvious and are very tempting. They can be mistaken as friends! After recognizing the enemy, the teacher points the weapon (non-attachment) to be used in order to destroy the foe to realization. After understanding fully what lies ahead, the disciple must pursue his objective, the Primal Purusha (the root of the Asvattha-tree) with absolute dedication.*
>
> *We are also given a hint about the nature of the world and*

its origin by using the example of the Asvattha-tree. The implication is that the world as we know it is a replica of something substantial elsewhere. What we call the Unmanifest and manifest are now referred to as the implicate and explicate by physicists.

5) Free from pride and delusion, with the evil of attachment conquered, ever absorbed and contemplating on the Self, their desires being completely stilled, liberated from the pairs of opposites known as pleasure and pain, the undeluded reach that eternal Goal.

Comment: The qualification necessary to reach that Goal is now presented for the benefit of the aspirant. Pride is the foremost of them which has to be overcome. It leads to misperception (delusion) between good and evil, and attachment to the objects of desire. One must be free from the attraction of pleasure and the other side of it which is pain. These are the nooses that bind the Self, and the disciplines mentioned in the verse prior to this are the means to become liberated from them.

6) There the sun illumines not, nor the moon, nor fire; that is My Supreme Abode. By going there, they return not.

Comment: This is an extraordinary description of the Goal to be achieved by following the disciplines. The Abode of the Lord does not depend on the galaxies or anything else we know. That is the eternal Abode, on reaching which one does not return to this world of death.

7) An eternal portion of Myself having become the Jiva in the world of Jivas, attracts the senses, with mind as the sixth, abiding in Prakriti.

8) When the Lord obtains a body and when He leaves it, He takes these subtle organs and goes in the same way as the wind carries the scents from their sources.

9) Presiding over the ear, the eye, the touch, the taste, and the smell, as also the mind, He experiences objects.

10) The deluded do not see him who departs, stays and enjoys, who is conjoined with the Gunas, but they see who possess the Eye of Wisdom.

11) Those who strive endued with yoga, cognize Him dwelling in the Self; though striving, the unrefined and unintelligent see Him not.

> *Comment 7-11: The Jiva is the embodied Being in this world, consisting of the subtle and causal bodies, the senses etc. A part, not a piece, of the Lord dwells in them – because the Lord cannot be divided. It is mentioned elsewhere that the Lord sustains the whole universe with a single atom of Himself.*
>
> *It is the Lord that experiences, not the physical body. At the time of death, the Lord leaves the body and takes with Him all the stored up experiences. A Self-realised person only can know this. The means by which this can be known is yoga. Unless the nature of a person is refined, he cannot understand the true nature of what happens. Therefore, it is necessary to follow the principle (sadhana) in order to experience one's Divine Self.*

12) The light which residing in the sun illumines the whole world, that which is in the moon and in the fire – know that light to be Mine.

13) Entering the earth I support all beings by My energy; and having become the sapid moon I nourish all herbs.

14) Abiding in the body of living beings as Vaisvanara, associated with Prana and Apana, I digest the four kinds of food.

15) And I am seated in the hearts of all; from Me are memory, knowledge, as well as their loss; I am verily that which has to be

known by all the Vedas; I am indeed the author of the Vedanta as well as the knower of the Vedas.

> *Comment 12-15: The Lord first explains that by His Presence He maintains the Orderly Solar System and the whole Creation. From Him memory comes because He is unchangeable. He is also the Source of Knowledge, the One Who knows the Vedas and to be realised by Vedic studies. By proclaiming that He is the author of Vedanta, the Lord gives a stamp of authority to the highest Wisdom.*

16) There are two Purushas in the world – the Perishable and the Imperishable. All (manifest) beings are the Perishable, and the Kutastha is called the Imperishable.

17) But distinct from these is the Supreme Purusha, called the Highest Self, the indestructible Lord, who pervades and sustains the three worlds.

18) As I transcend the Perishable and am even above the Imperishable, therefore am I known in the world and in the Veda as 'Purushottama', the Highest Purusha.

> *Comment 16-18: The perishable Purusha relates to the relative form of existence which we normally attribute reality to. The Imperishable is another state of existence in which everything subsists after the dissolution of the material world and on which all are dependant for their individual existences. This Absolute is known as the Supreme Purusha or Supreme Self in the Vedas.*

19) He who is undeluded knows Me as the highest Self. He knows all, O Bharata, and worships Me with his full heart.

20) Thus, O sinless one, this most profound teaching has been imparted by Me. Whoever knows this becomes enlightened, O Bharata, and he has reached the fulfilment of all his duties.

Comment 19-20: In conclusion, the Lord says that whoever is freed from ignorance will know Him as the One really worthy of worshiping, and refers to the above discussion as the most competent for making a person enlightened. It is important to note that this achievement comes by steadfast practising of one's duties and not just by living in caves or the performance of rituals. This emphasis on duty is not generally recognized by Vedantists as means to liberation. Their emphasis is on knowledge only and this has got a negative impact on society by encouraging people to relinquish their responsibilities. Arjuna wanted to do the same, but Krishna strongly urged him against it. Elsewhere Krishna said that a person is free from duties when he finds delight only in the Atman.

CHAPTER SIXTEEN:

The Yoga of division between the Divine and the Demonical

1) The Blessed Lord said: Fearlessness, purity of heart, steadfastness in knowledge and yoga, almsgiving, control of the senses, Yajna, study of the scriptures, austerity and straightforwardness;

2) Non-injury, truth, absence of anger, renunciation, serenity, absence of denigration, compassion to all beings, uncovetousness, gentleness, modesty, non-involvement in frivolous activities.

3) Vigour, forgiveness, fortitude, purity, loving, humble, these belong to one born for a Divine state, O Bharata.

4) O Partha! Ostentation, arrogance and self-conceit, anger and also harshness and ignorance are the qualities by which one is born for a demoniac state.

> *Comment 1-4:* The characteristics of a saintly person have been here well defined. Anyone without these characteristics cannot claim to be saintly. This is a workable definition for those aspiring to find a spiritual person. Persons with these characteristics are the friends of the world.
>
> Those who are claiming a saintly status, but behave otherwise, are the enemies of this world. They use religion as a means to exploit the innocent. These people of demonic nature use the media and other means to make a show of themselves in order to attract the ignorant and take advantage of their innocence.

The Yoga of Division – Divine and Demonical

5) The Divine nature, O Pandava, is favorable for liberation, the demoniacal is conducive to bondage; grieve not since you are of a Divine nature.

> *Comment: The destiny of those with Divine and demonic natures has been clearly defined according to the science of the Gunas. Lord Krishna admonishes Arjuna not to worry because he does not fit into the demonic category.*

6) There are two kinds of beings in this world. One is the Divine and the other is demonical. The Divine has been described at length. Hear from Me, O Partha, of the demonical.

7) The demoniac do not know what to do and what to refrain from; neither purity, nor right conduct nor truth is found in them.

8) They say: "The Universe is unreal, without a moral basis and God. It is born only out of mutual union and brought about by lust. Nothing else."

9) Holding this view, these ruined souls of little intelligence and fierce deeds, rise as enemies of the world for its destruction.

10) Filled with insatiable desires, full of hypocrisy, pride and arrogance, holding evil ideas through delusion, they work with impure resolve;

11) Beset with immense cares that only end in death, and regarding the gratification of lust as most important, they are convinced that all else are of no value.

12) Bound by a hundred ties of hope and overtaken by lust and anger, they strive to secure by unjust means hoards of wealth only for sensual enjoyment.

> *Comment 6-12: The verses above, mentioned two categories of people – those who are virtuous and those who are evil. A*

detailed account is also given about the perverse nature of those who are evil. It is a good presentation of the conditions we are living in today. This knowledge is necessary in order to avoid getting involved with those of evil intent.

13) "This today has been gained by me; this desire I shall fulfill; this is mine, and this wealth also shall be mine in future.

14) "That enemy has been slain by me, and others also shall I slay. I am a lord, I enjoy, and I am successful, powerful and happy.

15) "I am rich and well-born. Who else is equal to me? I will sacrifice, I will give alms, I will rejoice." Thus deluded by ignorance;

16) Bewildered by many a fancy, enmeshed in the snare of delusion, addicted to the gratification of lust, they fall into a foul hell.

Comment 13 -16: Evil people think and plan for their own selfish satisfaction at the cost of others. Their ignorance and arrogance lead them to self-destruction, not before causing much harm to others. That is why they are called demon which means those who cause suffering to others.

17) Self-conceited, obstinate, filled with pride and intoxicated with wealth, they perform sacrifice ostentatiously only for name by disregarding the Sacred Law (Dharma).

18) Given over to egoism, power, insolence, lust and wrath, these malicious people hate Me in their own bodies and those of others.

19) Those malicious haters, worst among men in the world, I hurl these evil-doers for ever into the wombs of the demons only.

20) Entering into demoniac wombs, these deluded ones, birth

The Yoga of Division – Divine and Demonical

after birth, thus fall, O Kaunteya, into a condition still lower, without ever reaching Me.

21) Triple are the gates that lead to hell, destructive of the Self. They are lust, anger and greed. Knowing these three as such, one should therefore reject them.

> *Comment 17-21: After enumerating the natural tendencies of the evil-doers, the Lord ascribes these to be of three basic characteristics – lust, anger and greed. These drive men mad by creating an imbalanced mind, which causes them to behave abnormally. And with this diabolical attitude they cause the Lord to suffer in their own body and in the bodies of others. But ultimately they destroy themselves.*

22) The man who is liberated from these three gates to damnation, O Kaunteya, practises what is good for him and thus achieves the Supreme Good.

> *Comment: Since these are the basic causes of man's problem, it is only after overcoming them that he can work towards his own salvation and for the good of the world.*

23) He who rejects the ordinances of the scriptures and acts on the impulse of desire, attains not perfection, nor happiness, nor the Supreme Goal.

24) Therefore, let the scriptures be your authority in deciding what you ought to do and what should not be done. Having known what is said in the ordinance of the scriptures, you should act accordingly.

> *Comment 23-24: Not by following impulsive desire one can attain what is good for him, but by following the precept of the scriptures which declare in no uncertain terms that one must not do what is harmful to another – and anyone who does otherwise is doing so by violating the ordinances of the*

scriptures. These principles are based on the insights of the wise, are full of logic and are convincing. Let them be the guide of what to do and what should not be done.

CHAPTER SEVENTEEN:

THE YOGA OF THE THREEFOLD SHRADDHA

1) Arjuna said: What is the nature of the devotion of those, O Krishna, who, though disregarding the ordinances of the Scriptures, perform sacrifice with Shraddha? Is it of the nature of Sattva, Rajas or Tamas?

> *Comment: Arjuna's question is quite pertinent. It relates to the fact that some people follow certain practices to suit their own purposes by ignoring the principles laid down in the Scriptures or one may say: twist the meaning of the scriptures to suit their own purpose. He wants to know under what category such practices fall although they are done with devotion. There is a strong emphasis in religion on belief which implies that one should be submissive to whatever is taught without questioning. Arjuna's query relates to a rational approach to religion. A good teacher like Krishna encourages it because a good explanation removes any confusion that might be in an aspirant's mind.*

2) The Blessed Lord said: The Shraddha of all beings is of three kinds, in accordance with their nature – they may fall under one of these categories, Sattvika (pure), Rajasika (passionate), Tamasika (negative). Hear now about them.

3) The Shraddha of every man, O Bharata, is in accordance with his natural disposition. Man is of the nature of his Shraddha; what his Shraddha is, that verily he is.

> *Comment 2-3: Krishna makes a very important observation*

and the principles of yoga are based on this understanding of the personality of every individual, which falls under one of the three basic categories of the Gunas. The attitude of every individual is in accordance with his own character. What his character is that is what he is. In life, there are so many things one can lose. But if he loses his character, he has lost everything. Therefore, one's foremost duty is to improve one's character by practising what is good and ignore all things that are harmful.

The Sanskrit word 'Shraddha' is often translated as 'faith' and Krishna mentions three categories of it. It is worthwhile mentioning that faith can be negative as well through misguidance or natural disposition, in which case it poses itself as religion but acts against the sublime principles of religion. Faith and belief are two different things. Belief comes by what one is taught, but faith is the natural disposition of a person and it falls under three different categories. It can be evil as well.

4) Sattvika men worship the Devas; Rajasika, the Yakshas and the Rakshasas; the others – the Tamasika men – worship the Pretas and the hosts of Bhutas.

5) Those men who practise fierce kind of austerities that are not enjoined by the scriptures, given to hypocrisy and egoism, impelled by the force of lust and attachment,

6) Foolish as they are, they torture their own bodily organs, and Me also who dwell within them – know them to be Asurika in their resolve.

Comment 4-6: Those of pure nature worship the Divine, those who are full of passion worship the Yakshas and the Rakshasas (demi-gods and demons) and the others worship the Pretas and Bhutas (spirits of the dead and ghosts). And the Lord repeats again how these foolish people torture themselves and the God that dwells in them.

The Yoga of the Threefold Shraddha 159

7) The food also that is dear to all is of three kinds and so are the Yajnas, austerities and gifts. Listen now to the distinction of them.

8) The foods that enhance vitality, energy, vigour, health, joy and cheerfulness, which are relished for its value and naturally agreeable, substantial and agreeable, are liked by the Sattvika.

9) The foods that are bitter, sour, saline, over-hot, pungent, dry and scorching are liked by the Rajasika. They produce pain, grief and disease.

10) That which is stale, tasteless, rotten, cooked overnight, refuse and impure is the food liked by the Tamasika.

> *Comment 7-10: It is normally thought that a person who performs sacrifices practises, austerities and makes gifts is of a religious nature. Krishna makes a wise distinction by stating that these fall under three categories and in accordance to a person's natural disposition. This distinction takes into consideration, not only the act but the motive behind the act. Some may appear to be doing good things but there may be some hidden selfish motive behind that appearance. And it is the motive that makes all the difference.*
>
> *A person's choices also are based on his natural disposition which has been categorized under the kinds of food that is liked. Lord Krishna warns us to beware of likes and dislikes in making choices. Most often we think that the things we like are what is good and our decision is generally based on that. However, between likes and dislikes is the good. Our choice must be based on what is good whether we like it or not.*
>
> *We are all known by our habits but usually we do not give much consideration to our food habits. Here Krishna is warning us that wrong food habits affect us physically, mentally and spiritually. In order to improve our nature we need to take the foods that are healthy for body, mind and*

> *spirit. The world is beginning to realise that the healthiest food is vegetarian. The wise amongst us are going back to the ancient teachings. But conditioned by long habits, even when knowing the truth, there are others who try to justify their wrong habits in which they find pleasure! Ultimately they pay the price for their negative pursuits.*

11) That Yajna is Sattvika which is performed by men desiring no fruit, as enjoined by the rules, with their mind concentrating on the Yajna only, for its own sake.

12) O best of the Bharatas! Know that Yajna to be Rajasika which is performed with the expectation of a reward or for self-glorification.

13) They declare that Yajna to be Tamasika which is contrary to the ordinances, when no food is distributed and which is devoid of Mantras, gifts and Shraddha (pure faith).

> *Comment 11-13: Yajnas performed by the three categories of men are clearly noticeable in society. Virtuous people perform Yajna for its own sake without expecting any reward and are blessed by the Lord. They do not make a show. Most people follow the crowd and by so doing ignore the ordinances of the scriptures while others look to how much they will be rewarded for the performance of the rites and make a show of what they are doing. The fruit of such sacrifices though immediate, are temporary being performed for materialistic advantages.*

14) Worship of the Gods, of the twice-born, of teachers and of the wise; purity, uprightness, continence, and non-injury – these are said to be the austerity of the body.

15) The speech which causes no excitement, which is truthful, pleasant and beneficial, and also the practice of sacred recitation – these are said to form the austerity of speech.

16) Serenity of mind, gentleness, silence, self-control and purity of disposition – this is called the mental austerity.

> *Comment 14-16: There are three instruments of action: body, speech and mind. These instruments make the world what it is. If they are used as mentioned above, this world can be a happy place. These characteristics represent the nature of good men. When these instruments are used indiscreetly, much suffering is caused. Therefore, the emphasis is on good conduct.*

17) This threefold austerity practised by steadfast men with the utmost Shraddha, desiring no fruit, they call Sattvika.

18) The austerity which is practised with the intention of gaining respect, honour and reverence, and with ostentation is said to be Rajasika; it is unstable and transitory.

19) That austerity which is practised with a foolish obstinacy, with self-tortures or for the purpose of destroying another, is declared to be Tamasika.

> *Comment 17-19: This distinction of those who perform penances helps the seeker to understand that not everything that meets the eye is perfect and there is a need to be analytical in order to select that which is right. Of the three different characteristics of men undertaking penances, the virtuous are those who renounce all rewards. Most of them do it for the sake of honour, respect and reverence, and among them all is an evil group that undertakes any amount of tribulation in order to destroy others. They are the thorns of the world; or else the world is a beautiful place in which everyone can enjoy peace and happiness.*

20) That gift which is made to one who can make none in return, with the feeling that it is one's duty to give, and which is given at the right place and time and to a worthy person, that gift is held as Sattvika.

Comment: The highest ideal of what constitutes charity has been presented here over five thousand years ago. If this is followed, the world will be free from poverty and conflicts. Charity must entirely be made to deserving persons or causes, without the motive of getting anything in return. The objective, then, is to give help, so that the beneficiary will overcome the problems facing them. That help must be given unconditionally. If nations were to adopt this principle, a friendly relationship would develop that would have a great deal of economic advantage to all. We only have to think of the amount of money that is spent on armaments because of the distrust there is among nations. Lord Krishna's message is not for individuals only. It is for the whole of mankind. It is spirituality in action, not a system of beliefs based only on prayer and worship.

21) But that gift which is given with a view to receive something in return, or looking forward for the fruit, or given grudgingly, is regarded as Rajasika.

Comment: The word 'Rajasika' is derived from the word 'Raja' or King. In this context there is a sense of pride and egotism and more often than not, charity is made with a personal motive that is calculating. Even in ancient times this was looked upon by the Rishis as more mean and harmful than beneficial. Charities are often made with the Rajasic motive, especially by those missionaries who expect people to be converted to their religion by offering services or financial benefits.

22) That gift is declared to be Tamasika which is given at a wrong time or place, or to unworthy persons, without respect or with insult.

Comment: When gifts are made to undeserving persons or causes, with a grudging attitude and at a wrong time and place, it is an expression of the low character of the giver. Such gifts are of little value to the giver as well as the receiver because of the degenerate motive. The negative inclination by which the gift is made follows the giver and in the end devours him.

23) 'Om Tat Sat': this has been declared to be the triple designation of Brahman. By that were made of old the Brahmanas, the Vedas and the Yajnas.

24) Therefore, the scriptures declared that with the utterance of 'Om', sacrifice, gift and austerity are always undertaken by the followers of the Vedas.

25) By uttering 'Tat' without seeking any fruits, sacrifice and austerity and the various acts of gifts are performed by those aspire for Moksha.

> *Comment 23-25: Om Tat Sat represent the triple primal characteristics of Brahman the Absolute, the Source from which were derived the Vedas with its attributes, Brahmanas which consists of sacrifices. Hence the authority of the scriptures.*
>
> *From the scriptures we get the teachings of what should be done and what should be avoided. Since Om is one of the characteristics of Brahman, every gift gets impregnated with cosmic power when Om is repeated while making it. This act purifies the giver, the gift and the receiver. This sanctification brings about prosperity, peace and happiness to the giver as well as the receiver and the cause for which it is made.*
>
> *When Tat is uttered in any sacrifice, austerity and making of gifts, the performer must contemplate on the attainment of Moksha or Liberation, because such mental attitude purifies the undertaking. While performing such, the mind must be focused on the highest achievement of life's purpose – then the greatest good is achieved. One must always aim at the highest in pursuit in life. Such aspiration brings out the best in one's nature.*

26) The word 'Sat' is used in the sense of reality and of goodness; and so also, O Partha, the word 'Sat' is used in the sense of an auspicious act.

27) Steadfastness in sacrifice, austerity and gift is also called 'Sat' and services for the Lord is called 'Sat'.

> *Comment 26-27: The word 'Sat' (which means 'existence') includes all acts that are positive and is one of the primal characteristics of the Absolute (Sat-Chit-Ananda). Therefore, it includes all the other auspicious acts mentioned earlier. It is important to note that the qualities of commitment, the spirit of sacrifice, generosity and service to the Lord are of paramount importance.*

28) Whatever is sacrificed, given or performed and whatever austerity is practised without Shraddha, it is called Asat, O Partha. It is of no account here or hereafter.

> *Comment: In this respect 'Shraddha' means 'inner urge'. This human life has a special purpose which is to attain Liberation. If there is a lack of an innate urge to elevate oneself, then it is likely that one will forfeit this human birth in the next life. That is what is meant by 'no account here or hereafter'. According to the Vedic tradition there are two paths that men aspire to follow. By one they go never to return. By the other they go and return again. But those without any aspiration neither go nor return like the lower form of creatures. It is to them that this reference is made. The objective is to encourage one to look at life very positively rather than procrastinating endlessly. Life itself is a challenge, which must be faced both discreetly and courageously.*

CHAPTER EIGHTEEN:

THE YOGA OF LIBERATION BY RENUNCIATION

1) Arjuna said: I desire to know in detail the truth of Sanyasa, O Hrishikesa, and also of Tyaga, O slayer of Kesi.

> *Comment: Arjuna wishes to know the real difference between Sanyasa and Tyaga because there is a subtle difference between the two and one can be mistaken for the other.*

2) The Blessed Lord said: The Renunciation of Kamya Karma, the sages understand as Sanyasa; the wise declare relinquishing the fruits of all work as Tyaga.

3) Some sages declare that all action should be given up as evil, while others say that Yajna, gift and austerity should not be relinquished.

> *Comment 2-3: Renunciation in its true sense does not relate to physical action. A sanyasin must have control over the active mind. He must free the mind from desires and enjoy the bliss of peace. So long as the mind is full of desires it will remain restless. After one has renounced the material world, there should be no desire for material things. In the first instance it is the awareness of the impermanence of material things that induces one to live a life of renunciation. But this can be easily forgotten in the process of ease and comfort.*
>
> *Renunciation of the fruit of action is known as Tyaga. While some believe that all actions should be given up as evil, others*

maintained that Yajna, gifts and charity should not be given up.

4) Learn from Me the truth about Renunciation and Tyaga, O best of the Bharatas; Tyaga, verily, O best of men, has been declared to be of three kinds.

5) Acts of Yajna, gift and austerity should not be given up. They should be performed because they are purifying to the wise.

6) But even these actions should be performed without attachment to the fruits, O Partha. This is My certain and best belief.

7) Verily, the abandonment of any obligatory duty is not proper. Such abandonment out of ignorance is declared to be Tamasika.

8) He who abandons action out of fear of physical hardship or because it is painful is performing a Rajasika abandonment and obtains no fruit thereof.

9) Whatever obligatory work is done, O Arjuna, merely because it ought to be done and when it is performed without attachment and desiring of fruit, that denial is deemed to be Sattvika.

10) The renunciate imbued with Sattva and a steady understanding and with his doubts dispelled, does not hate unpleasant work, nor is he attached to one that is pleasant.

> *Comment 4-10: After stating the general opinion about Renunciation, the Lord gives His views on the subject. Renunciation of the fruits of action falls under three categories. Although the performance of sacrifice, the offering of gifts and austerity must not be given up – because of their purifying effects – yet they must be done with a spirit of detachment. Otherwise, they also will loose their positive values.*

Man is dependant on so many things for his survival and therefore he has an obligation to these things. It is for his benefit that he must take care of the sources he depends on for his livelihood.

All obligatory duties relating to the family, the society, the country, etc. are to be performed. No duty is high or low and a person's esteem does not depend on the kind of duty he performs but how he executes it. The man of high character and pure nature does not choose between what is pleasant and unpleasant, but rather chooses what is good and necessary. In this respect a sweeper who does his job properly is better than a King who does not manage his affairs well.

The worldly man always assesses the value of a work on the basis of its remuneration. According to his judgment even the most difficult work becomes simple if it is properly paid for! The Rajasic relinquishment of work because of its difficulty, rather than thinking of it in terms of necessity, is the materialistic way of thinking which creates more problems than it solves. The world is made up of more people with this attitude. Hence the dissatisfaction, which is one of the main causes of many problems.

11) It is indeed impossible for an embodied being to renounce action entirely. But he who renounces the fruit of action is regarded as one who has rightly renounced.

12) The threefold fruit of action – evil, good and mixed – accumulates after death to one who does not relinquish but there is none ever for the one who renounces.

Comment 11-12: Only a dead man cannot do anything. The functioning of the organs of the body is itself a form of activity. And the maintenance of them requires one to act. Since it is impossible to do without activity and it is considered by some that it is the cause of attachment, Krishna proposes that one should apply the principle of detachment from the fruit of action, and He considers this as the truest form of renunciation. Moreover, by following this principle one is able to perform better than when one is attached since one is able to avoid the stress factor that causes so much physical and mental problems.

Every action has a threefold effect and these accumulate in the life of a man who is attached to them, and he takes them over even to his next life. But the man who is unattached is liberated from them and enjoys a state of freedom and bliss. This is the reward that one achieves by not clinging to rewards!

13) Learn from Me, O mighty-armed, the five factors which relate to the accomplishment of all actions as taught in the Samkhya (philosophy) and which lead to the end of all actions.

14) The body, the agent, the various senses, the different functions of various kinds, and destiny or accumulated karma as the fifth.

15) Whatever action a man may perform with his body, speech or mind – whether right or wrong – these five are its causes.

16) Failing to recognize this, the man whose mind is tainted, owing to his imperfect understanding and totally distorted perception looks upon the absolute Self as the doer.

17) He who is free from egoism and whose understanding is not tainted – though he kills these people, he kills not, nor is he bound.

Comment 13-17: After mentioning the categories of action according to the teachings of the Sage Kapila, who had a profound understanding of man and the reasons for him behaving in a particular way, the Lord then enumerates the instruments through which all actions are accomplished and the

> means to their end. The benefit of this teaching is the understanding that action is not only performed by the body, but by other non-physical instruments as well.
>
> Krishna draws our attention to an even more important fact. The actions performed by the instruments are usually attributed to the Supreme Being. This lack of proper understanding is due to one's perverse nature. But a man of realization who is detached from these instruments, even if he kills, he does not commit a sin, neither is he affected by its consequence. However, as mentioned elsewhere, since a man of realization neither hates nor causes another to hate, it is impossible for him to kill unjustly if at all he kills. And the implication is that violence is committed by those who are egoistic and ignorant.
>
> We may cite an example of a police-officer who pursues a criminal. In the process the criminal may try to kill him. If the officer in defense kills the criminal, he is not charged for murder because he did what was expected of him while performing his duty. In this case although he kills, he is not looked upon by the public as a killer.

18) Knowledge, the object of knowledge and the knower form the threefold inducement to action; and the instrument, the object and the agent are the threefold constituents of action.

19) Knowledge, action and actor are declared in the science of the Gunas to be of three kinds only, according to the distinction of Gunas (qualities); hear of them also as they are.

> Comment 18-19: Krishna goes deeper into discussing this abstruse subject about action. He clarifies that we are not free agents. We are induced into action by the influence of Gunas that make up our nature. It is not something external to us but our second self.

20) The knowledge by which the one Imperishable Being is seen in all existences, undivided in the divided, know that knowledge to be Sattvika.

21) But that knowledge by which one sees in all beings as manifold entities of different kinds as varying from one another – know that knowledge to be Rajasika.

22) And the knowledge that clings to one single effect (a part) as if it were the whole, and is without reason, not based on truth, and is trivial – that knowledge is declared to be Tamasika.

> *Comment 20-22: Actor, action and the knowledge which the actor applies to perform an act are of three categories. The Absolute is indivisible and knowing that to be so is Pure Knowledge. This kind of knowledge leads to love, friendship, harmony, peace and happiness.*
>
> *The other kind of knowledge is that which sees everything as having separate existences and from this understanding comes the problem of wanting to possess, dominate, oppress, etc. This kind of understanding has been the basic cause of adverse human relationships and problems from the time of Creation. There has been and continues to be war after war leading to all sorts of human suffering.*
>
> *Another form of defective knowledge is mistaking a part for the whole. This has a particular reference to dogmatic religions that claim to be the only and truly valid way to salvation, having disregard for every other system as degenerate and invalid. This misunderstanding of a part as the whole results in evangelization and conversion, and we know the result of this negative attitude only too well. Since dogma by its very nature is exclusive, it can not logically claim to be complete. And to do so is due to ignorance.*

23) An action which is preordained is free from attachment and

which is done without love or hatred by one not desirous of the fruit, that action is declared to be Sattvika.

24) But that action which is done by craving for desires, or again with egoism, or with too much effort, that is declared to be Rajasika.

25) That action which is undertaken from delusion, without heeding the consequence, loss, injury and ability, that is declared to be Tamasika.

> *Comment 23-25: Preordained actions are those related to previous lives and have connection with reincarnation. According to this theory, no one is entirely free. He has brought a 'baggage' from previous lives and to the extent that this has control over his present action, he is excused. This generosity is not generally known and many people think of the Law of Karma as something that demands its 'pound of flesh'. The other part is to act with a balanced mind — free from the influence of love or hate or the expectation of a reward. These acts are of the highest order. They bring joy to everyone.*

26) An agent is called Sattvika who is free from attachment and egotism, endowed with firmness and zeal and unaffected by success or failure.

27) An agent is said to be Rajasika who is passionate, desirous of the fruit of action, greedy, cruel, impure and affected by joy and sorrow.

28) One who is unsteady, vulgar, stubborn, deceitful, malicious, indolent, despondent, procrastinating — such an agent is called Tamasika.

> *Comment 26-28: The man of pure nature is free from attachment and egoism, firm in his decision and pursues what*

> has to be done. He focuses his mind on the cause for which he acts and does not get influenced by success or failure.
>
> The second category is a replica of actions we see in an unstable society: passionate, full of desires that force him to act indiscriminately, causing him to be greedy and cruel. A person of such impure nature is always tempted by temporary joy that leads him to deeper grief.
>
> The third category is that of ignorance. This refers to one who causes suffering to others and disregards the consequences that will have upon himself. He is driven by malice and hate that ultimately leads to senseless destruction and suffering. It also makes people docile and careless.

29) Hear from Me the threefold distinction of understanding and firmness, according to the Gunas, as I explain them exhaustively and numerically, O Dhananjaya.

30) The intellect which makes a distinction between the paths of work and renunciation, right and wrong action, fear and fearlessness, bondage and liberation – that intellect, O Partha, is in the Sattvika state.

31) O Partha! That intellect is in the Rajasika state when it makes a distorted grasp of Dharma and adharma (what is good and what is evil), what ought to be done and what ought not to be done.

32) Know it to be in the Tamasika state when it is enveloped in darkness and, regards adharma as Dharma, and views all things in a perverted way.

> *Comment 29-32:* Krishna now gives a more thorough explanation of how one's understanding and resolution are affected according to one's natural disposition.
>
> That intellect which is able to grasp correctly what is right and

The Yoga of Liberation by Renunciation

> *wrong, and what really is work and what is renunciation, etc., is of a pure state, and to recognize one of an impure mental state who looks at things in a distorted way. The other refers to one who perceives things contrariwise, because he is in a state of utter ignorance.*

33) The unswerving firmness by which, through yoga, the functions of the mind, the Prana and the senses are regulated, that firmness, O Partha, is Sattvika.

34) But the firmness, O Arjuna, by which one holds fast to Dharma, Kama and Artha, desirous of the fruit of each from attachment, that firmness, O Partha, is Rajasika.

35) That stubbornness, O Partha, is Tamasika by which a stupid man does not give up sleep, fear, grief, despair and also conceit.

> *Comment 33-35: Here is a further categorization of firmness because it can be misplaced and be the cause of suffering unless it is applied wisely. When it is used as a means to control the senses, the life energy and the mind, it is considered to be of the highest order.*
>
> *Even firm attachment to religious values is looked upon as flawed when considered from the point of view of attaining Moksha, which is the highest goal of life. The other goals are relative and although important, if one sticks with them, one misses the true purpose of life. This can be better understood when one looks at the traditional four stages of life that finally lead to sanyasa or renunciation.*
>
> *The third kind is obstinacy by which one cannot perceive what is good or harmful for oneself and indulges in everything that is negative and refuses to admit that one is wrong in spite of all the good advice. Ravana, of the Ramayana is an apt example.*

36) And now hear from Me, O chief of the Bharatas, the three

kinds of happiness by which a man comes to rejoice by long practice and in which he reaches the end of his sorrow;

> *Comment: After explaining so many categories of valuable teachings, Krishna now speaks about something that deludes everyone. We all think of happiness as anything that gives a pleasant feeling. But Krishna is defining happiness into three different categories and understanding of this can make life quite different.*

37) That which is like poison at first but like nectar in the end is said to be Sattvika, born of translucence of the intellect due to Self-realization.

38) That happiness which arises from the contact of the senses and their objects, and which is like nectar at first but like poison at the end is known as Rajasika.

39) That happiness which deludes the self both at the beginning and at the end and which arises from sleep, sloth and miscomprehension – that is declared to be Tamasika.

> *Comment 37-39: The happiness which one attains through long practice of discipline and austerity and which leads to Self-realization is real happiness. It is the end of all sorrows. It does not depend on an external factor. It comes from the liberation from all conditioning – physical and mental.*
>
> *The other is pleasure which one gets from external objects. Material objects are sources that make one eternally dependent. In the beginning there is temporary enjoyment. But that leads to frustration and suffering in the end. That is the way of the worldly. The wise do not take interest in it.*
>
> *The last of them is the pleasure one gets by not living at all – one who is attached to sleepy habits and to whom the world does not seem to exist!*

The Yoga of Liberation by Renunciation

40) There is no being on earth, or again in heaven among the Devas, that is free from the three Gunas, born of Prakriti.

> *Comment: The Lord wants us to know that the scientific principle of the Gunas pervades everything that exists – not only man. Everything in the Universe operates on the basis of the principle of the Gunas. Even the guardian Deities are subject to them.*

41) The duties of the Brahmanas, Kshtriyas and Vaisyas as well as Sudras, O scorcher of foes, are divided according to the Gunas of their inborn nature.

> *Comment: This verse refers to the social orders of society. There has been a division of labor for the proper functioning of society for the good of all. This division of duties into four categories has been done according to the inborn tendencies of individuals who were formed into groups known as teachers, soldiers, policemen to protect the country and the law, merchants and tradesmen, and laborers. This is known as the 'caste-system' which has been blamed for the division of society. Originally, there were four castes which were divided into a 'system' for an orderly functioning of the society. It was perhaps the first systematic division of labor into four categories to enhance productivity, to maintain law and order, to promote proper education and distribution of wealth according to one's need.*

42) Serenity, self-restraint, austerity, purity, forgiveness, and also uprightness, knowledge, realization, belief in a hereafter – these are the qualities of the Brahmanas, born of their own nature.

43) Heroism, vigor, firmness, resourcefulness, not retreating from battle, generosity and lordliness are the traits of the Kshatriyas born of their own nature.

44) Agriculture, cattle-rearing and trade are the duties of the Vaisyas in accordance to the inborn tendency of their own nature;

and action consisting of service is the
accordance of the inborn tendency of th

Comment 42-44: Here, the duties of
defined and this indicates that society u
those early times as it is today. Yet, we ca
of those four categories is still maintaine
standards materially. But it is doubtf
standards of those early periods have b
that been so, we would have had more
basic problem seems to be that moral pro
with technical development.

45) Each devoted to his own duty attain
Hear how a man attains perfection by fo

46) He, from whom all beings evolve
pervaded, worshiping Him with his own duty, man attains perfection.

47) Better is one's own Dharma, though imperfect, than the Dharma of another well performed. He who performs the duty ordained by his own nature incurs no sin.

48) One should not abandon, O Kaunteya, the duty to which one is born, although it is associated with blemish. In reality, all undertakings are connected with some kind of defect even as fire is by smoke.

Comment 45-48: The objective of the duties is not merely for acquiring material objects but the stress is on moral perfection in order to attain Self-realization. With Self-realization as the basic objective of life, every act has to become sanctified in the process of daily living. It gives value to every act whether it is easy or difficult. One's preferences based on material reward are to be considered as 'sinful' because they create competitive and unstable societies, giving the strong the power to take advantage of the weak.

The word 'blemish' refers to disadvantage. Not everything we do may appear to be for our own personal advantage. At times we have to make sacrifices for the good of others. That is the way to maintain a harmonious society. If we apply the same principle to nations whereby the richer ones contribute to those who are not so fortunate, the world would be a different place. Certainly there would be fewer conflicts.

Moreover, there is the understanding that the Divine is present in all activities. Hence every act is sanctified by that Presence, and adoring Him through our activities leads to self-perfection. This has been the ideal that guided human conduct in ancient times.

49) He whose intellect is unattached everywhere, who has restrained his conditioned self and is free from desire, by renunciation he attains the Supreme State of freedom from action.

Comment: By maintaining a detached attitude through the effective performance of one's duties, a state of freedom is attained when one is no longer attached to action. This is the secret of the Gita's message. We start by renouncing the fruit of action and end up with non-attachment to any particular action.

50) Learn from Me in brief, O Kaunteya, how reaching such perfection, he attains to Brahman, that supreme consummation of knowledge.

51) Endowed with pure understanding, restraining the self resolutely, withdrawing from sound and other objects, and aloofness to attraction and aversion;

52) Dwelling in solitude, eating just little, with speech, body and mind constrained, always engaged in meditation and concentration, with dispassion;

53) Having abandoned egoism, violence, arrogance, desire, enmity, property, free from the notion of 'mine' and peaceful, he is fit for becoming Brahman.

54) Becoming Brahman, serene-minded, he neither grieves nor desires. Being the same to all beings, he attains supreme devotion to Me.

55) By devotion he knows in truth What and Who I am; then knowing Me in truth, he forthwith enters into Me.

> *Comment 50-55: Krishna explains that non-attachment leads to purity of one's nature and then comes revelation through knowledge. The principles are set out by which there is a transformation that results in the mortal becoming immortal. That is the Supreme State when one sees the Lord dwelling in all beings. After reaching that state he is constantly in communion with the Lord. That communion leads to union with the Lord which is the highest state. After reaching that state a person is not born again, as he reached the ultimate goal of his earthly existence.*
>
> *It is important to understand that we first start with commitment to duty and from this commitment mental stability develops and our nature becomes more in tune with the spiritual. After fulfilling our obligations to the world and we become older, we are naturally more devoted to the pursuit of Self-realisation.*

56) Continually doing all actions and taking refuge in Me, by My grace he reaches the eternal un-decaying Abode.

57) Mentally surrendering all deeds to Me, regarding Me as the highest goal and resorting to Buddhi-yoga, do you ever fix your mind on Me.

58) Fix your mind on Me. By My grace you will overcome all obstacles. But because of egoism, if you do not listen to Me, you will perish.

59) If filled with egoism, you think: 'I will not fight', vain is your resolve. Your nature will compel you.

60) Bound by your own nature-born karma that which from delusion you wish not to do, even that you shall do helplessly against your will O Kaunteya.

61) The Lord dwells in the hearts of all beings, O Arjuna, and by his Maya (illusive power) causes all beings to revolve as though mounted on a machine.

62) Seek refuge in Him alone with all your heart, O Bharata. By His grace you will gain Supreme Peace and the eternal Abode.

> *Comment 56-62: Finally, Krishna sums up in a most profound way what He has said earlier and tells Arjuna to take heed of what He has told him, because his nature will force him to act in spite of what he thinks. Nature does not operate on its own. It requires the Presence of the Lord to be able to take refuge in Him and win His grace, so that one can overcome one's negative tendencies and attain peace.*

63) Thus, wisdom more profound than all profundities has been declared to you by Me. Reflect upon it fully and act as you choose.

> *Comment: As the dialogue comes nearer to conclusion, Krishna declares to Arjuna that he has been given the greatest of all teachings and asks him to assess carefully what he has been told then to make up his own mind about what he should do. That freedom must have had a great impact on Arjuna because Krishna was speaking most convincingly about what he should really do, even from the beginning of the discussion. Yet, there was no compulsion on the part of Arjuna to follow His advice. This attitude of Krishna is most remarkable and sets a noble example of the spirit in which a dialogue should proceed. It leaves no room for unfriendliness in the end.*

64) Listen again to My supreme word, the profoundest of all. You are beloved of Me and steadfast of heart; therefore I shall tell you what is good for you.

65) Fix your mind on Me; be devoted to Me; sacrifice to Me; prostrate before Me; by so doing you shall come to Me. This is My pledge to you, for you are dear to Me.

66) Renounce all Dharmas (duties) and take refuge in Me alone. I shall liberate you from all sins; grieve not.

67) This is never to be spoken by you to one who is devoid of austerities, nor to one who is not devoted, nor to one who does not do service, nor to one who speaks ill of Me.

> *Comment 64-67: Earlier, the Lord told Arjuna about the people who are dear to Him. Now He is talking directly to him about their special relationship. And because of that relationship, He is going to reveal to him the most precious of His teachings. He asks Arjuna to take complete refuge in Him and assures him that He is going to protect him. Arjuna is very fortunate to have that privilege.*
>
> *It appears that so far Krishna's teaching is general. Now His teaching is particularly for Arjuna, who was in a confused state of mind regarding his duties. Krishna then says to him to renounce all his duties, something He was advising him all the while not to do. But then there is a caution that this must not be taught to everyone. He mentions the character of those who are worthy to receive that teaching. Otherwise people may quote Him as saying that social duties are not important and that would bring about degeneration of society. Elsewhere He gives a warning that if He does not do anything, people will follow His example and that will ruin the whole world.*

68) He who with supreme devotion to Me will teach this

immensely profound philosophy to My devotees, shall doubtless come to Me alone.

69) Nor is there any among men who renders dearer service to Me than he; nor shall there be another on earth dearer to Me than he.

> *Comment 68-69: To those who are qualified, i.e. those who live an austere life, are full of devotion and perform selfless service – nothing is more rewarding than propagating the teachings of the Bhagavad Gita – not those who do nothing more than talking. To Him they are dearest. It is good to put into practice what Krishna has taught, but better is one who also propagates what has been taught. This is the real message – apply, realise and propagate. This is the way to transform the whole world, to make our world a better place, a heaven here on earth.*

70) And he who will study this sacred dialogue of ours, by him I shall have been worshiped by Jnana Yajna; such is My conviction.

71) And the man who hears this, full of faith and free from derision – even he, liberated from evil, shall attain the auspicious regions of the righteous.

> *Comment 70-71: The teachings of the Gita are of relevance to others as well. Here is an encouragement to study the Teachings and not to accept them dogmatically. The reward of such study (scientific and philosophical analysis) leads to the worship of Krishna through the Path of Wisdom. Elsewhere, Krishna says there is no difference between the Jnani (the man of wisdom) and Himself. Those who listen to the teachings – full of faith in them – are free from sins and attain the abode of the virtuous. But the man of wisdom is His very Self. This pursuit of Pure Knowledge appears to be one of the central teachings of the Gita, and is consistent with the message of the Vedas.*

> We should note here that the Gita urges us to aspire to attain the highest goal of life. And that goal is attained not only when one is free from evil deeds but one must transcend what is good as well.

72) Has this been heard by you, O Partha, with an attentive mind? Has the delusion of your ignorance been destroyed, O Dhananjaya?

> Comment: These are the final words of the Lord on the battlefield of Kurukshetra. The questions are short and direct. All through the dialogue, Arjuna was asking the questions. Now Krishna asks: "Did you listen to what I said with a concentrated mind? Are you now free from all your misconceptions?"
>
> The first step to learning is to learn to listen. Unless one listens attentively nothing can be learnt. Very few people can listen with concentration for a long time. Arjuna has that special characteristic.
>
> In the Mahabharata, it is mentioned that after the children of the Pandavas and Kauras finished their studies under Dronacharya, he finally gave them a test relating to their power of concentration, because concentration is necessary for success in all aspects of life.
>
> On top of a tree was placed a doll bird and one after the other, they were told to aim their arrow at the eye of the bird. Except Arjuna, the others failed because their concentration was not steady. This shows that to learn to concentrate was an important part of the syllabus in ancient times.

73) Arjuna said: My delusion is destroyed. I have regained my memory through Your grace, O Achyuta. I am firm; I am free from doubt. I shall act according to Your word.

> Comment: The impact of the knowledge expounded by Krishna

destroyed all the doubts that were in Arjuna's mind. After being fully satisfied with the answers to his questions, he submits to Krishna that he would act according to His direction, i.e. to carry out his duties and responsibilities according to the principles of Dharma.

74) Sanjaya said: Thus have I heard this wonderful dialogue between Vasudeva and the high-souled Partha which caused my hair to stand on end.

75) Through the grace of Vyasa have I heard this supreme and most profound yoga directly from Krishna, the Lord of Yoga Himself declaring it.

76) O King, as I recall over and over this wonderful and holy dialogue between Kesava and Arjuna, I rejoice again and again.

77) And as often as I recall that most wondrous form of Hari, great is my wonder, O King, and I rejoice again and again.

78) Wherever is Krishna, the Lord of Yoga, wherever is Partha, the wielder of the bow, there assuredly are prosperity, victory, expansion, and sound policy; such is my conviction.

> *Comment 74-78: Sanjaya was placed in a fortunate position to witness the whole episode. After expressing what the impact of the dialogue had on him, he finally gave a very brief and significant comment. Those few words are worthy to be taken noticed of, because they come from one who had the direct vision, and as we were assured in the very beginning of this dialogue, whatever he says would be true.*
>
> *He speaks of the Gita's message as the combination of Power and Wisdom. With such a combination there will be PROTECTION, PROSPERITY AND PROGRESS. To my mind that is exactly the purpose for which Lord Krishna had taken birth in our troubled world. He wanted to establish the rule*

of Divine Law (Dharma) so that the whole of Creation can enjoy this earth and not only a chosen few. This message is perhaps more relevant today than when it was delivered on the battlefield of Kurukshetra.

APPENDIX

Chapter VIII 17-19

The number of sidereal years embraced in the foregoing different periods are as follows:

	Mortal years
• 360 days make a mortal year	1
• Krita Yuga consists of	1,728,000
• Treta Yuga " "	1,296,000
• Dwarara Yuga " "	864,000
• Kali Yuga " "	432,000
• The total years of the four Yugaa make a Maha	4,4320,000
• Seventy-one Maha Yugas form the period of reign of one Manu	306,720,000
• The reign of 14 Manus equals 994 Maha Yugas	4,294,080,000
• Add Sandhis i.e. intervals between the reign of each Manu which amount to 6 Maha Yugas	25,920,000
• The total of these reigns and intervals between the 44 Manus is 1,000 Maha Yugas which equals to a Kalpa or a day of Brahma	4,320,000,000

Alice A. Bailey comments that these figures are not fanciful, but are founded upon astronomical facts, have been demonstrated by Mr. Davis, in an essay in the Asiatic Researches; and this receives further corroboration from geological investigations and calculation made by Dr. Hunt, formerly President of the Anthropological Society, and also in some respects from the researches made by Professor Huxley.

Great as the period of the Maha Kalpa seems to be, we are assured *that thousands and thousands of millions of such Maha Kalpas have passed, and as many more are yet to come. (Vide Brahma-Vaivarta and Bhavisya Puranas; and Linga Purana, ch. 171, verse 107, &c.) and this in plain language means that the Time past is infinite and the Time to come is equally infinite. The Universe is formed, dissolved, and reproduced, in an indeterminate succession (Bhagavad Gita, VIII: 19 – The Theosophist. Vol. III, p. 115)*